SAINT BENEDICT AND HIS MONKS

SAINT BENEDICT
AND HIS MONKS

Theodore Maynard

This book is set in Monotype 'Garamond' series

NIHIL OBSTAT:

JOANNES M. T. BARTON, S.T.D., L.S.S., Censor deputatus

IMPRIMATUR:

E. MORROGH BERNARD, Vic. Gen.
Westmonasterii, die 24a Septembris, 1955

Made and printed in England by
STAPLES PRINTERS LIMITED
at their Rochester, Kent, establishment

TO THE
RIGHT REVEREND PATRICK O'BRIEN, O.S.B.
ABBOT OF ST MARY'S
NEWARK, N.J.

Contents

Preface

SHORT as this book is, I have endeavoured to present not only what biographical facts we have concerning St Benedict but some account of his Rule and its significance, indicating something of Benedictine history through the centuries, not neglecting the influence of the Benedictine spirit upon Catholic life today. I prescind altogether from any analysis of the sources or the philology of the Rule, except in so far as my readers may be referred to the learned authors by whom such matters are discussed. My sole object is to do something useful for the average person who wants a general idea of such matters. It is not my expectation to contribute anything new, though I hope to avoid baseless conjectures and impermissible conjectures. As the experts do not always agree with one another, they are not likely to approve of all that I write. It will be enough if I do not wholly fail in the modest object I set before myself.

One of the main things to note and always hold before ourselves is that St Benedict's career occurred just at the time the old Roman Empire was collapsing. Monte Cassino was on the main road between Rome and Naples but was left undisturbed, at the moment apparently not affecting the course of world events but unconsciously preparing an instrument that was soon going to affect them most decisively. As contrasted with this, a Protestant historian of monastic origins, Mr James O. Hannay, remarks that

interesting and beautiful though the life in the Nitria or
the Thebaid may have been, the monks of the Desert had as
little importance to the history of Egypt as 'if St Anthony
and his disciples had inhabited the forests of Germany or
the plains of Russia.' Whereas another Protestant historian
of the subject, Dr Herbert B. Workman, pointing out that
in the Latin Empire, especially in Italy, 'individualism, pure
and simple, had but slight chance of survival,' attributes
the orderliness attained to the all but universal acceptance
of the Benedictine Rule. It was the monastic institution
as remodelled in the West by Benedict that provided the
stability which was the prime requisite of a society in
well-nigh complete disruption. That it was able to do so
was because the distinguishing feature of the Holy Rule
was that it demanded stability of the monks themselves.

The process took a long time. As Abbot Butler writes
in his classic *Benedictine Monachism*: 'There was a Europe
to be reconverted, christianized, civilized anew; law and
order to be restored; the fabric of society to be rebuilt; the
dignity of labour to be reasserted; agriculture, commerce,
education, the arts of peace to be revived; civil and political life to be renewed; in short, a Europe to be remade.'

St Benedict had never envisaged the part his monks
were to play in this colossal undertaking. At first he had
simply left the world, despairing of it as hopelessly evil
and wishing only to contemplate God, living as a hermit
in a cave. Even when in the providence of God he emerged
from this to reorganize monasticism, he and his monks
lived entirely cut off from all the world's concerns. But
though he had no wish to do anything except establish a
school for God's service, what he provided, quite beyond
his designs (though he would have fully approved of
what his monks were eventually called upon to perform),

was an instrument for the regeneration of society. The extraordinary thing is that he was able to forge this weapon – a gentle, permeating spirit rather than a sword – during times when everything apparently operated against the success of his idea.

There are two, and only two, sources for the life of St Benedict – the Second Book of the *Dialogues* of St Gregory the Great and the Holy Rule – and neither can be considered as giving much of the kind of information for which a modern biographer looks. As even St Gregory is almost always vague about dates, Benedictine scholars are forced to inferences, which, naturally, vary widely. They are, however, unanimous in regarding the verses of Mark the Poet on Benedict as not belonging to the period to which they purport to belong, and in dismissing the *Life of St Maurus* as an eighth-century forgery. Nevertheless, a number of more or less useful hints may be derived from this or that ancient writer, though these have to be used with caution; and fortunately we know a good deal about the times in which St Benedict lived and especially about the development of early monasticism. Our greatest good fortune of all is that in recent years the whole field has been investigated by a number of brilliant and able men – perhaps the best of whom have been English Benedictines – so that though many minor points remain uncertain, a clear enough general picture has emerged.

It is, however, to St Gregory that we are obliged to go for the life of Benedict. Though it may well be true, as has often been suggested, that Gregory wrote of Benedict primarily because of his fame as a thaumaturgist, almost completely ignoring the features that a modern biographer would stress, this great monk – the first Benedictine to become Pope – was certainly far from being unmindful

of the importance of the monastic reconstruction that
Benedict effected and did much to further its extension.
Furthermore, he showed, by sending Benedictine monks
as missionaries to England, that he was fully aware of
the instrument providentially put into his hand.

Moreover, the *Dialogues* are not completely devoid of
biographical information, but contain all that we have
that is reliable, meagre though this is. And the miracles
commonly are accompanied with conversations between
Gregory and his Deacon, Peter, that are not only often
full of literary charm, but which serve to illuminate the
fatherly character of the wonder-worker. Without these
conversations the book would have been bare indeed. As
it is, the record of a miracle recorded of any saint often
tells us next to nothing about the man himself, as exactly
the same thing might have been related of other saints,
and similar things often are. So, too, with the Holy Rule:
though Benedict never permits himself autobiographical
reminiscences, we may find these sometimes by reading
between the lines, as the personality of the man shines
through the monastic legislator. Indeed, we may find
more about what kind of person Benedict was in the
Rule than in the *Dialogues*.

However, all this, though it places the biographer under
a handicap, involves him in no embarrassment. St Gregory
is too cautious to commit himself to statements that might
be challenged and provides no more than the kind of
general outline that wears every appearance of plausibility.
It would be well for us to bear in mind certain facts: one is
that even if the seventh century was no doubt in some
ways uncritical, we would be very foolish to suppose that
it contained a higher proportion of gullible people than
are found today; another is that Gregory the Great was a

man of affairs, who had served as papal ambassador to the
Court of Byzantium before becoming Pope; finally, the
title of 'the Great' was given to him for excellent reason.

In what Gregory the Great tells us about Benedict he
very carefully cites his authorities. With one exception all
were very old men – Benedict's successors as abbots –
and from these he had received no written statements but
merely oral information. The exception, an important
one, is that of one of his own subdeacons, Florentius, the
grandson of the wicked priest of the same name at
Subiaco, from whom he may be presumed to have obtained information that was known only to the family.
But there was nobody at all who could have given first-
hand information about Benedict's early years, so what we
hear about that part of his life could have come to us
merely as what scraps aged monks might have remembered as having been related about Benedict's boyhood.

In any account of the life of St Benedict, many dates,
though not the facts themselves, must remain largely
conjectural. A widely accepted tradition is that he was
born about 480 and died about 547, though each writer
modifies slightly according to his own judgment. The most
startling divergences are those proposed by Abbot Chapman in his very brilliant *St Benedict and the Sixth Century*,
for he thinks that the Saint lived until 553 or a year or
two later, and suggests several other dates that do not
accord with what has been usually supposed. For example,
he gives reasons for his belief that the arrival at Monte
Cassino was earlier than the traditional date, and that the
same is true of the composition of the Holy Rule. None of
this, of course, is susceptible of definite proof but is based
upon the weighing of probabilities. At the moment at least
it is enough for us to accept tradition as serviceable.

At the risk of being invidious I make mention here of some of the works given in my bibliography. Dom Philibert Schmitz's *Histoire de l'Ordre de Saint-Benoît* I found useful rather than inspiring. But of the many commentaries on the Holy Rule, some of them going back to quite early times, the one used by me, and which will undoubtedly prove most serviceable to readers of today, is that by Abbot Paul Delatte of Solesmes, as translated in 1921 by Dom Justin McCann. Formerly Master of St Benet's Hall, Oxford, Justin McCann has been titular Abbot of Westminster since about 1950. He published his *Saint Benedict* in 1937, and in 1951 brought out his edition of the Rule in Latin and English, a production of the highest value. His book on Benedict, if perhaps not so dazzling as the more erudite and specialized study by Abbot Chapman, may be taken as the best for ordinary use; I have drawn upon it heavily. Another English abbot, Cuthbert Butler, has given a remarkable interpretation of the Benedictine spirit and Benedictine history. Even those who do not agree with him at all points agree as to his forthright honesty, as will everybody who ever knew him.

I would like to add a work of thanks to the Very Reverend Matthew Hoehn, O.S.B., Prior and Librarian of St Mary's Abbey, Newark, New Jersey, for the loan of many indispensable books, and to the Reverend Bonaventure Schwinn, O.S.B., editor of the *American Benedictine Review*, for his reading of the manuscript and the suggestions he made.

THEODORE MAYNARD

Port Washington,
August 15, 1954

One

The Early Life of the Saint

BENEDICT WAS BORN in 480 at Nursia, a small town among the Sabine Hills. The old-fashioned and somewhat rugged virtue of these mountaineers was proverbial: Cicero had called the Sabines *severissimi homines*, and those of Nursia – *Nursina durities* – were regarded as the most austere of them all. It was from this place that had come such men as Sertorius and Vespasian, veritable embodiments of qualities rarely to be found in their time.

We do not know positively the name of Benedict's father and mother, but all the indications are that they were rather well-to-do, perhaps we might say members of the small provincial gentry. There have even been biographers – though not recent ones – who have been so bold as to supply an almost complete family tree, or at least to claim that there was a close connection between Benedict's family and the illustrious and immensely wealthy Anicians. The whole thing seems to be due to nothing but the desire of old-style hagiographers to provide their subjects, whenever possible, with an exalted lineage.

We do, however, have two names associated with his youth. One is that of Scholastica, whom tradition makes Benedict's twin. She became a nun, apparently first living at home, as was common enough at that time in the case of religious women, but is subsequently known to have

lived at a hermitage or convent which is usually located at
Plumbariola, about three miles from the foot of Monte
Cassino. We do not hear of her except in the charming
story of the last meeting between brother and sister,
which was within a week or two of the death of them
both. But it may be surmised that Scholastica had more
than a little to do with Benedict's resolve to leave the
world and to become a monk.

Scholastica is mentioned only at the very end of Benedict's life. One who appears at its beginning was Cyrilla,
described as the 'nurse' who accompanied the youth
when he went to Rome to complete the education begun
at Nursia, as likely as not under a tutor who was a slave. If
this is the case, it might explain why the latter did not
accompany Benedict to Rome, for students of good
family customarily took their tutors along. On the other
hand, if Cyrilla was really only a nurse – one pictures a
'nanny' for a small boy – she may have gone on account
of his youth. She may also have gone to see that he be-
haved himself, but though there are indications that
Cyrilla was a pious woman – one who may have helped to
develop his piety – there are also indications that the
youth had reached an age when the control of a woman
like Cyrilla could not have accomplished much. That
Benedict himself was pious from his earliest years is not
to be doubted; it may be inferred that this was because of
the upbringing he had received from his father and
mother, and they may have felt that he would be safer in
Rome, where he was likely to encounter moral dangers,
if he had somebody like Cyrilla at hand. But the inference
is that her function was that of a housekeeper rather than
that of a nurse, as we understand the term.

It has been suggested that while in the city Benedict

resided either in the Anician palace or in a hostel attached to it. All that may be safely said is that he took some sort of an apartment and that Cyrilla looked after it, keeping a motherly eye on him, preparing his meals and mending his clothes. She is most unlikely to have been qualified to perform any of the functions of a tutor. It is clear that he did not consult her about the new plans he was soon to make and that she merely accompanied the young master, as in duty bound, for as long as this was permitted.

Benedict's infantile piety is stressed even in the opening words of the Second Book of the *Dialogues*: 'During his boyhood he showed mature understanding, and a strength of character far beyond his years kept his heart detached from every pleasure. Even while still living in the world, free to enjoy all it had to offer, he saw how empty it was and turned from it without regret.' The way in which that is put sounds faintly priggish and therefore not very attractive. What pleasures could a boy have had at his disposal except play and occasional skylarking, and these would have been good for him. Even had he enjoyed a few extra dainties to eat, that would have been natural and innocent. One does not wish the young to have premature gravity. In any event, St Gregory could not have known anybody able to testify to such things from personal knowledge, and we may be quite sure that Benedict would never have spoken of himself in such terms, though he may (and probably did) say in later life that he had been strictly brought up in a devout Christian family, from which it could have been inferred that he had always been a well-behaved child. Priggishness is about the very last trait that we find exhibited in the Holy Rule when it came to be drawn up. Therefore we may deduce from the wise and tolerant man, with his dislikes of extremes or any singularity, but occasional touches of mild humour, that much the same qualities were in him during his youth. One fears that at least here St Gregory was introducing his hero in the terms of conventional hagiography.

As to how old Benedict was when he went to study at Rome there has been a good deal of conjecture, for we can do no more than draw what seems to be the most suitable inference from what Gregory the Great tells us. It used to be surmised that the boy was there from the time he had finished his elementary studies, which would probably be about fourteen. The reason for this supposition is not at all clear, unless it was taken for granted that Cyrilla was literally his nurse, only in that event why could he not have remained at home, for surely Nursia would have been able to supply his early educational needs?

The Rome of that day was still a city of magnificent buildings, but from what we hear of it in connection with Benedict it is clear that it was also a wicked city in spite of its nominal Christianity, and that this wickedness did not exist merely in the minds of strait-laced provincial parents. There it stood, glorious in buildings of marble and bronze, despite the scars suffered from barbarian invasions, among which the newer Christian churches (except when they were remodelled pagan temples) made no very splendid showing. Yet Christianity was hardly more than a veneer laid over the corruptions of the past, and the official class was almost solidly Arian. As for paganism, though in practical form it was widespread even in Rome, few except the illiterate now openly professed it, for the very word 'pagan' meant rustic, indicating that only an untaught peasantry were faithful to the ancient gods. The discovery that Rome, though it was the centre of the Christian world, was actually far from being Christian was a distinct shock to the strictly schooled youth from the Sabine mountains. Yet mingled with that instinctive recoil he felt a fascination which he perceived to be dangerous.

Though no Benedictine scholar claims to have any certainty about the matter, the consensus of opinion among modern scholars today is that Benedict went to Rome not as a schoolboy but as a university student, that is, at about the age of seventeen or eighteen. On the face of it, such a supposition is more likely than any other. Just what he studied has to be deduced, in so far as this is possible, from what we find in his sole literary production, the Holy Rule. Yet this is not altogether a safe guide because, even if Benedict had been a university student when he arrived in Rome, and therefore would not have had time to get very far in his studies, he nevertheless, during subsequent years, was able to make good his deficiencies by a course of private reading. What we learn from the Rule is that though his reading had been wide, he mainly draws upon the Scriptures, the Fathers, and the written regulations of his monastic predecessors. From this it must not be too confidently asserted that he confined himself to such works, only that these would have yielded what was most suitable for his purpose. Yet despite the fact that he now and then drew upon the literature of ancient Rome, the probability is that Benedict had done no more than dip into this.

We have a solid reason for thinking so, for if he had ever followed the course of liberal studies, which was almost wholly concerned with the Greek and Latin classical writers, this does not come out in what he himself wrote. His own Latin was of the popular sort, which has sometimes been rather unfairly described as 'low', or even, occasionally, as ungrammatical, or what might have seemed so to one who had been ground through the mill of the *eruditio liberalis*. It has sometimes been suggested that Benedict deliberately adopted this style in order to make himself understood by the people of his own day. But though it was undoubtedly the way in which people ordinarily spoke and wrote, his monks at least would have had no difficulty in arriving at his meaning had he written with attention to literary graces. Such graces need not have involved the mere flourishes and the kind of fantastic triviality then too often in vogue. To my mind, therefore, it seems clear that Benedict did not receive what we would call the ordinary literary education, else this would have manifested itself. It may well be that he had a fortunate escape, for not only was he always direct and simple and to the point, but his character was devoid of the stamp of any affectation that would have spoiled him for the work he was destined to do.

For much the same reasons it would seem most unlikely that he entered any school of rhetoric, for in all these was practiced a mode of declamation that gave much more attention to style than to substance. These schools may have had more solidity than a purely literary course of studies, in so far as the great forensic authors were pored over and analysed, but they also went in for a good deal of speechmaking and debating about matters little related to actuality, and artifice and gestures and perorations were given more than their due weight. Such a course of studies would have spoiled Benedict as surely as would the *eruditio liberalis*. It need only be said here that, while he does give evidence now and then of having read the authors of antiquity, nothing could be less rhetorical than the Holy Rule he was to write.

There is a third possibility, and one that is more likely, though the evidence for it cannot be considered quite conclusive. It is that Benedict entered a law school, since one encounters in many parts of the Rule a legal terminology. Yet this may be accounted for as springing from the nature of the writing, for while the Rule has a fatherly intimacy about it, it is primarily a piece of legislation, a code. Nevertheless this possibility should not be pressed too far. Benedict's studies, in whatever department he enrolled, were not exhaustive, if for no other reason than that he suddenly decided to terminate them. He could conceivably have picked up a certain number of legal tags, even a certain amount of legal jargon, in later years. There are those who go so far as to suggest that he wrote with the Code of Justinian before him, and others suggest that the case is the other way around. As neither theory is susceptible of proof, I suggest that Benedict had entered a law school at Rome.

In any event he did not remain very long, for what he saw of the prevalence of vice among the students made him retreat, 'knowingly ignorant and wisely unlearned'. It may even be that he thought the city more wicked than it was, for one may easily imagine that there was then (as there is now) a type of student whose idea of fun is rather crudely to instruct an innocent country lad in the 'facts of life'. Whatever it was that happened, Benedict was so shocked that he made up his mind to become a monk.

Several disparate things may be adduced from what St Gregory tells us. First of all, no doubt, must be placed the fact that Benedict wished to preserve his innocence. That he took refuge in flight indicates that he did not fail to feel the seductiveness of the evil he now first learned of, even though startled and appalled by its first impact. He may also have preferred to remain ignorant – the term is only relative – of the kind of studies taught during a rather frivolous age, his serious nature and common sense perceiving them to be largely waste of time. It may have seemed to him, even had he completed his studies and won prestige as a lawyer or politician, that it would only have been to win a worldly success that was dangerous for his soul. Above all – though about this St Gregory says nothing, for he could have known nothing – it may have been that the serious consideration Benedict was at this time forced to give to a number of new problems drove him deeper into himself and therefore deeper toward God.

In acting as he did – and one would gather that Benedict was only about eighteen – the question arises as to whether he received parental permission. As his studies may have lasted longer than Gregory the Great would seem to suggest, and as Nursia was not very far from Rome, he could have gone home now and then and discussed his problems with his father and mother. However, there is no indication that he gave them the slightest inkling of what was in his mind. It may be that, excellent Christians though they were, they would have urged him to continue with his studies, adding some advice as to how best to guard himself against the evil that prompted his decision. But it may be that it was precisely because he knew just what his father and mother would say that he told them nothing, but simply disappeared.

St Gregory writes of his giving up his inheritance, and this could have been accomplished by an agreement reached after he had buried himself in a cave as a hermit and so needing nothing more from the world. It could also mean that he was disinherited by a sternly disapproving father. But probably St Gregory was only writing in general terms, without any definite information. For while there is nothing to show that any great fortune came to Benedict, even after his father's death, he may still have received his patrimony and it may have been relatively small. The only other person so far as we know who could have inherited would have been Scholastica, and if the whole of the family wealth was bequeathed to her, it is likely that one who so thoroughly shared Benedict's religious enthusiasm would have seen to it that his share of the family fortune was not permanently lost to him. In any event, it is evident that when later the need for them arose, Benedict, whether at Subiaco or Monte Cassino, was not lacking in benefactors. It is quite possible that in the matter of the renounced legacy we are ingeniously inventing a problem that does not exist.

At the same time, the way the matter is presented to us in the *Dialogues*, one gets the impression that Benedict left Rome without any explanations to those who had every right to them – an action that cannot be called altogether praiseworthy. But this may be merely because St Gregory had no information to give and did not want to speculate. However, had Benedict wished to go to Nursia to disclose his plans he would have taken the road that runs along the Tiber Valley as far as Reate and then continued along the Salarian Way that ran only a little south of where his parents lived. Instead, he took the Valerian Way due westward and then, for unexplained reasons, struck southward to Enfide, passing, as he did so, the Subiaco with which he was to be long associated. That he did so strongly suggests two things: that he was not yet perfectly clear in his mind as to what he was going to do, and that he deliberately avoided a visit to Nursia.

It may be he had heard something of the Church of St Peter at Enfide and of the hospice attached. What St Gregory says is simply that 'a number of devout men in-

vited them to stay there and provided them with lodging
near the Church of St Peter'. It has been conjectured –
and at this stage of Benedict's story we are obliged to
reconcile ourselves to conjectures – that in the hospice
lodged a number of men who studied with the local priests
with the intention of themselves entering the priesthood.
Abbot McCann tosses out the apparently contradictory
suppositions that the stay at Enfide was merely temporary,
as Benedict had formed at Rome the intention of becoming
a monk, and that after staying awhile at Enfide he began
to wonder if perhaps he could not find monastic peace
without going any farther. Others, like Abbot Herwegen,
having hinted that he might have received clerical ordination at Enfide and might have laid there the foundation of
his knowledge of the Fathers. Of course there were no such
things as theological seminaries in those days – or until
after the Council of Trent – but this may have been as
close an approach to one as could be found. If so, was it
necessary that Cyrilla remain with him as his housekeeper?
    One would gather from Gregory the Great that the
stay here was short – at most only a few months, and not
long enough to have permitted Benedict to progress
very far in his theological studies. Though Cardinal
Schuster argues, on rather flimsy evidence and against the
whole weight of Benedictine tradition, that Benedict became a priest, it is most unlikely that he would have been
ordained at Enfide, if it ever did happen. He may have
received minor orders, as a mark of his ultimate intention,
but even of that there is not the slightest proof. As for his
supposititious priesthood, this must be summarily rejected, as St Gregory would have been sure to have mentioned the fact, if it had been one. Moreover, the whole
tenor of the Holy Rule takes it for granted that monks

would be laymen under an abbot who was also a layman.

That it is perhaps difficult for a monk of our own time to visualize such a situation may be the reason that Abbots Cabrol and Herwegen harp upon the possibility of Benedict's having received at least the diaconate. If this (or the priesthood) had been received it would hardly have been at Enfide, but at some stage in his later life. However, the objection remains that this is never mentioned, obliging us to accept the consensus of opinion that it never happened. As for Benedict's knowledge of the Fathers having been acquired at Enfide, he had plenty of time for this before he composed the Holy Rule.

Just as Benedict departed suddenly from Rome, though he was enrolled there as a student, so there was also a sudden departure from Enfide, which suggests a very impulsive man, one very unlike the calm, benignant Benedict we usually think of. Though for the most part he is characterized by a serene prudence, he does, it is true, occasionally show in the stories related of him in the *Dialogues*, and even in the Rule itself, a touch of asperity. But the departure from Enfide raises a little problem, for it would seem that Benedict left without a word of explanation to Cyrilla, who apparently had to find her way back to Nursia as best she could. However, it may be that Benedict had some money with him and that he gave it to her to use on her journey, or even that he arranged for an escort. On the other hand, she may have preferred to remain where she was. If her status had been that of his personal slave, no doubt his last act would have been to give her manumission.

The occasion for this separation would seem to have been Cyrilla herself. She was the beneficiary of Benedict's first miracle, one that caused so much talk in the town

that his modesty could not endure it. 'Benedict,' says
Gregory, 'preferred to suffer ill-treatment from the world
rather than to enjoy its praises. He wanted to spend himself laboriously for God, not to be honoured by the
applause of men.' But indeed the applause was, both in
degree and quality, of a kind that might well have
embarrassed even one less self-effacing than Benedict.

What happened was this: Cyrilla had borrowed an
earthenware sieve from a neighbour, and had laid it on
the edge of a table from which it fell to the floor and broke.
Womanlike, she was in such distress over the trifling mishap that she was crying. Benedict himself felt so sorry for
the poor woman that he picked up the shattered sieve
and knelt praying with such earnestness that soon he, too,
was in tears. By chance he looked up: the two pieces of
the sieve had joined together; all the harm was mended.

Or so Cyrilla thought. She could not be expected to be
silent about a wonder of this sort, and as there was no
possible doubt as to what had happened, those connected
with St Peter's Church in Enfide hung up the sieve over
its door, where, as St Gregory tells us, it remained until
the time of the Lombards. The object aimed at was, we
may be sure, the fomenting of faith, but Benedict could
now never enter the church without seeing the sieve in its
conspicuous position, or being pointed out as the young
saint responsible for its presence there. This last bit was
too much for him, therefore 'he stole secretly away', not
knowing where he was going but merely looking for
some spot where he would not attract an attention
distasteful to him.

So far no false start had occurred in Benedict's life; but
after this we have to look at not one but two, and perhaps
even three periods in his career which may be regarded as

such, though in every instance he gained through them experience that equipped him all the better for what he was eventually to do. The better expression would therefore be preliminary phases. This time, as Benedict journeyed north-west along the bank of the river Anio, he had gone only about five miles when he was met by a monk named Romanus. The two got into conversation, and when Romanus found that the youth planned to become a hermit – presumably Romanus first suggested that the prospective hermit join his own monastery and had that suggestion rejected – he fell in with the idea that Benedict now had in mind, that of finding a cave nearby in which he could obtain complete seclusion without any danger of being pointed out as a wonder-worker. Romanus may even have helped him to pick out a suitable cave, as he knew the district well, and he certainly gave Benedict a monastic habit and promised to supply his simple needs as well as he could.

This habit was doubtless only a *melota*, or sheepskin garment of the utmost simplicity, perhaps with a hood, a garment such as the monks of the Desert used to wear, for there were as yet no religious Orders, as we understand the term, in which the garb is a kind of uniform. But the acceptance of it was regarded as binding Benedict to the religious state though no vows were taken; in fact, it does not appear that any vows were regarded as necessary by the monks of that time. All this, of course, was very far removed from the practice Benedict himself introduced a few years later when he abandoned the eremitical for the cenobitic life; still more, of course, is it at variance with the careful safeguards eventually introduced by canon law. Though even today there would be nothing to prevent a man from finding a cave and living there clad in a sheepskin, such a man would have no standing in the ecclesiastical system, nor would he be regarded as anything else but an eccentric. Furthermore, no monk who was not a superior of a community, and as such empowered to act officially, would have authority to admit another person into religion or to give him a habit of any kind. But it was evidently a permissible mode of procedure in those days. On top of everything else Romanus undertook to keep the whole matter secret.

Benedict selected a cave that was almost in the sheer wall of a precipice and, as such, all but inaccessible. It was near Subiaco and at the point where the river broadens out to make a lake, known in more ancient times as Sublacum. The lake had been formed, or enlarged, by a dam that the Emperor Claudius had built across the stream, and on this site Nero had erected a palace that was for him a country house, which one can imagine was crowded with concubines and courtiers with their wives and mistresses, gorging themselves on the disgusting banquets one associates with Nero's name. The ruins of that palace could still be discerned, and the dam built by Claudius remained until early in the fourteenth century when it was destroyed by floods. It was in this place of former lascivious luxury that Benedict, clad only in a shaggy sheepskin, and with nothing but the bare ground of the cave for bed and a stone for his pillow, gave himself up to the contemplation of the divine.

Such a life is one that modern men, even those of the deepest spirituality, find it hard even to picture, so completely has the religious life (at least in Europe) become communal, for even the Carthusians, who are basically hermits, live in a cloister. A life lived in absolute solitude in a cave must be either more or less than human, and most people would say it is subhuman. We have no record of what went on in Benedict's soul, but it should be supposed that, in so far as this is possible to mortal beings, it sought to remain in an unbroken communion with God.

The mature judgment that Benedict reached about the eremitical life appears in what he wrote many years later in the Holy Rule. Or rather in this is its carefully considered expression, for we find him reaching it only a few years after his first encounter with Romanus. He makes it clear that he does not withhold admiration from anchorites but added words that have to be taken as an admission that he had chosen his hermitage somewhat rashly. The words are: 'There are those who, not in the first fervour of their religious life, but after long probation in the monastery, having learned by association with many brethren how to fight the devil, go out well armed from the ranks of the community to the solitary combat of others, and by their own strength and God's assistance to fight against the temptations of mind and body.' He himself knew what he was talking about, for he had begun at the point which he continued to believe excellent, though only after monastic discipline as a preparation.

The abbey near Subiaco was under the rule of one Deodatus, and Romanus could do no more for Benedict than surreptitiously set aside a few scraps of bread from his own meagre allowance. This bread he used to tie in a cord and let the little bundle down the cliff, a bell being attached to let Benedict know that supplies were on their way. St Gregory tells us that one day 'the ancient enemy grew envious of the kindness shown by the older monk in supplying Benedict with food and so, while the bread was being lowered, he threw a stone and broke the bell'.

In spite of this, however, Romanus kept on with his
faithful service.

Regarding this incident one might venture to remark
that St Gregory is rather given to seeing the satanic hand
in almost any mishap. But though his explanation may be
as good as any other, the bell may also have been broken
by swinging against the rocky cliff in its descent. While
there is some reason for believing that Lucifer has lost a
good deal of his intelligence since his fall and is left with
little except cunning, it is difficult to suppose he would
be so stupid as to expect to ruin everything merely by
breaking a bell, though he may have done this by way of
venting his malice. At any rate, Romanus was able to
keep on with what he was doing, and little as was the
food that Benedict received, it sufficed to keep him alive.

This life went on for three years, and during all that
time Benedict never once left his cave, not even to hear
Mass or to confess himself or to receive Holy Communion. This was an extreme of individualism that
exceeded even that of the Desert, where the solitaries
gathered from their scattered abodes on Saturdays and
Sundays in the nearest church. Nobody is now exempt
from the ordinary law of the Church in such matters, or
has been for many centuries. But it was different then. It
was, in fact, so very different that we hear in Benedict's
story of a local priest who was just about to sit down to his
dinner on Easter Sunday when in a vision he saw (or
heard) something which rebuked him for preparing such
delicacies for himself while God's servant Benedict was in
the wilds suffering from hunger. Upon this the priest
sought the young hermit out – finding him at last, we are
not told how, unless it was that Benedict now and then
received visits from pious people, of whom this priest

had been one. Then, after some prayer and talk about the spiritual life, the priest brought out his little feast, saying, 'Today is Easter'. This was news to Benedict, so completely had he lost track of time. But he agreed that that was a day for a feast after the long Lent, so they ate their meal together, at the end of which, after some more conversation about the things of the soul, the priest left the cave and returned to his church.

Hidden as the cave was, it was not utterly concealed, for some shepherds (one imagines they were rather tenders of goats) wandering nearby caught sight of Benedict at the cave's mouth, half hidden by the thickets, and mistook him at first for some wild beast because of the sheepskin *melota* he wore. Drawing nearer, they found him to be a man and got into conversation with him and, brought under his charm, came again, bringing friends with them. From then on many people in the neighbourhood, recognizing his holiness, visited him and brought regular supplies of food. This was really the first indication we have that Benedict perceived that perhaps he was called to live a life of a different kind, one for the spiritual profit of the disciples who were seeking him out in increasing numbers.

He also was given an indication that the eremitical mode held special dangers for a young man, though just when the incident to be recorded occurred is not known. It seems that one day Benedict was powerfully assaulted by a temptation in the form of a little blackbird that fluttered around his face. He managed to catch the bird in his hands and, after making the sign of the cross, let it fly away. St Gregory hints that this was the devil in a rather unusual form. Immediately afterward Benedict was all but overcome by his memory of a woman he had once seen – no doubt during his student days in Rome – so that he nearly threw up his religious project then and there. Some have suggested that he was thinking of a girl whom he had known and of marrying her. But Abbot Cabrol remarks with great good sense: 'The question has naturally arisen: who was this woman whose memory after so many years of penance [actually it was at most three years] still haunted the mind of Benedict? All that can be discovered is unworthy of mention. What does it matter, after all? The woman is simply Woman: she is the temptation which tormented a St Anthony, and after him every solitary who, each in his turn, went through the critical hour in which his virtue was proved.'

In a case like this it seems hardly necessary to bring in any direct intervention of the enemy of mankind, for we all have a powerful enemy in our own flesh, and Benedict was at the age when the desires of the flesh are most clamant. What is more to the point than the blackbird (whose connection with the matter might have been quite imaginary) is the drastic cure that Benedict adopted. At the entrance to his cave there grew a thick patch of briers and nettles; therefore, throwing off his clothes, he flung himself among the thorns, rolling in them until his whole body was covered with blood. But the pain of the thorns and the smart of the nettles extinguished the desire he felt – so completely that, as he used to say afterwards, he was never again tempted in the same way.

St Gregory's comment upon the incident is that he was now the better able to instruct those who went to him for guidance. He adds the significant sentence: 'That is why Moses commanded the Levites to begin their service when they were twenty-five years old and to become guardians of the sacred vessels only at the age of fifty.' If Gregory means this to apply literally to Benedict, it would seem that he was now twenty-five, which would necessitate his having left Rome at a later age than anybody has yet suggested, or that he spent more than just a short time at Enfide; for he had remained in his cave only three years. But perhaps what Gregory wrote was only by way of illustration; if it is to be strictly applied to his chronology (and about this Gregory is usually rather vague), it would give us a clue not only as to how old Benedict was when he ceased to be a hermit, but perhaps also throw some light as to the date of the composition of the Holy Rule.

One other thing may be added to the thornbush story. There is a tradition that St Francis of Assisi many centuries later in the course of his journeys visited St Benedict's *Sacro Speco* and, finding the thornbush still there, blessed it, upon which it immediately burst into bloom. Cardinal Schuster adds – one supposes on the ground of his personal observation, for as a Benedictine he no doubt visited the spot – that not only is the thornbush still growing but that upon each of its leaves may be discerned what looks like the outline of a small serpent. The Cardinal says that this is probably only a caprice of nature, the mark left by a parasite; yet he confesses that it created in him a feeling of fear 'because it calls to mind the dread serpent which fourteen centuries ago slid over those thorns spewing his venom upon them'. Indeed, we do have cause to fear that Serpent; still more do we have cause to fear the concupiscence of our fallen nature. Few conquer it so decisively as the young Benedict.

In spite of himself his fame was growing and he was attracting disciples. Not merely was he visited by the local peasants and shepherds but important personages of Rome began to come to him. This gave offence to a priest in the neighbourhood named Florentius, for I take it that

B

the incident to be related occurred during the period of
Benedict's life in the cave though it could belong a year
or two later. This and another story about Florentius
receive substantiation from the circumstance that the
grandson of the priest (priests of the West could marry
as they still do among Catholics of the Eastern Rite
before receiving the diaconate) was one of St Gregory's
deacons, another Florentius.

It seems that the first Florentius conceived a hatred
of Benedict and started to spread calumnies about him.
It must be remembered that in those days a reputation for
holiness, such as had settled upon Benedict, conferred
some degree of spiritual authority even upon those who
had no official position, and this fact serves to explain
several things related of the Saint at various periods of his
life. St Gregory accounts for what happened on the
ground that Florentius himself 'would have liked to enjoy
the same reputation, though he took the greatest care
not to live the same life'. The animosity of this man
reached such a pitch that he tried to murder the young
anchorite who was exercising so much influence locally,
thereby detracting – or so Florentius imagined – from
his authority. Accordingly he sent Benedict as a Christmas
gift what was called an *elogium*, a loaf of bread blessed at
the Offertory at Mass. The loaf, however, was poisoned,
and Benedict suspected this, for he could not believe that
the gift was intended to express good will. Therefore he
called a raven that came to the cave to be fed from such
scraps as were left from the hermit's meagre meals, and in
the name of Christ told the bird to take the loaf and throw
it where nobody would be able to find it. The raven seemed
reluctant to obey, but eventually it did so, and upon
returning to the cave was given its usual portion of food.

Just how Benedict knew that the loaf was poisoned does not appear, unless it was by preternatural insight, but at all events he escaped the malice of Florentius that time.

That a priest should have been so carried away by the worst of feelings seems incredible, but it will be matched by something that happened not long afterward. One can only conclude that many so-called Christians, because of the rudeness and turbulence of the times and their own somewhat recent acceptance of the Faith, were in many cases just as bad as the pagans around them, and may even have had a darker tinge in their character that came from envy created by beholding a sanctity that rebuked their own disorders. But we need not flatter ourselves that we are really any better. Clearly the times had great violence about them, but where our refinement might shrink at the thought of committing murder, we may be more capable than they were of subtle sins; and we may lack the simplicity to revere holiness. At all events, it would seem that Florentius considered that what Benedict gained in authority was that much lost to himself, so he adopted this method of sweeping a rival from his path.

He failed with the *elogium* but he was by no means done with Benedict, though it was some time before he struck again. Meanwhile, it happened that a monastery not far away, at Vicovaro, which was about eighteen miles below Subiaco on the road to Tivoli, lost its abbot, and the monks conceived the idea that it would be good if they could obtain Benedict as their superior. Benedict did his utmost to evade this call, plainly telling the deputation of monks that 'their way of life and his would by no means agree', but as they were not to be put off he yielded in the end and went with them to Vicovaro as abbot.

Just what was the trouble he encountered there does

not appear. The monastery should have been sufficiently austere for anybody, judging from what may be seen of it – for it remains intact. It is nothing but a series of cells cut into the rock, each about six feet long and four feet wide, with no furnishings except two ledges on either side, one for a bed, the other to hold whatever clothing and similar articles the monks had. At the end of the row of cells is a refectory twenty-eight feet square, also cut out of the solid rock, with a stone table in the centre. On the lower level was the oratory, twenty-four feet long, at the eastern end nineteen feet wide but at the other narrowing to twelve. Yet more than austere surroundings are needed to make a good monk, and it soon became clear that the changes Benedict sought to introduce – changes that were no doubt along the lines of what he afterward developed in his Rule, emphasizing order on the one hand and on the other moderation – did not commend itself to these monks at all. It may have been that little regular work was done, and that the Divine Office was said in a slipshod fashion. It could even have been that the monks compensated themselves for their small cells by eating and drinking more than was fitting to their state, and that they wandered about pretty much as they wished. Whatever their irregularity, the young Abbot was firm, and the community sought to rid itself of him by bringing him at one of the meals a jug of poisoned wine. This, as was customary, he blessed while it was in the bearer's hands – and instantly the glass vessel was shattered.

At this Benedict rose in his seat and sternly addressed the cowering monks, saying: 'My brethren, may Almighty God have mercy upon you! Why did you treat me thus? Did I not tell you before that my ways and yours would never agree? Go then and seek an abbot according to your way of life, for me you can have no longer.' The point made here is that there was no generally accepted monastic rule but that monks lived then, as in many instances they did for some time to come, according to bits assembled from this rule or that (if they could be said to be rules at all), but mainly according to the improvised regulations of their abbot. Such a system had lamentably broken down at Vicovaro.

One might have thought that this initial failure – it was not, of course, Benedict's failure, though it might have been considered as such by those who did not know all the circumstances – would have given his prestige a damaging blow. The reason it did nothing of the kind must have been because the people in the locality were too well acquainted with the monks to be at all surprised at their refusal to be brought to heel, or because Benedict's reputation for sanctity was already too firmly established to suffer. So far from his being discredited, people flocked to his cave in increasing numbers, and the idea occurred to some of them that, if he could do nothing with a community hardened in its disorderly way of life, perhaps he might be persuaded to take charge of them, a group already partially indoctrined by him and whose docility was guaranteed.

To the pleas of local disciples were added those of highly placed Romans to whom his fame had penetrated. St Gregory tells us that now (or it may have been a little later) some of them begged him to take charge of their sons. Among them was the wealthy Equitius who asked him to accept a monastery in which he proposed to place his son Maurus – rather more than a boy but still quite young – and the Patrician Tertullus who offered his son Placid, who was still only a child. Even apart from requests of this sort it seems to have begun to dawn on Benedict that the time had come for him to leave the eremitical life and to proceed to the cenobitical. If Benedict had learned nothing else from the setback at Vicovaro it was what a community of monks living together ought to be.

He may also have perceived that he had proceeded in an inadvisable way: he had put the cart before the horse, he had tried to run before he could walk. No harm had been done in his particular case, but he made his views on the subject clear in the Rule. He saw that his mission was to give those flocking to him, or to the chosen ones among them, the training in the cloister he had come to see was normally indispensable to anybody who proposed to proceed eventually to the solitary life. He had himself, by God's grace, come through its dangers unscathed, but he recognized them to be serious. When he came to write his Holy Rule he may be said to suggest that a hermitage was a place to which one graduated, so to speak, after the training given in a community, though we have no record of any of his disciples leaving him for that higher life, if such it really was. Be this as it may, Benedict found himself unable to resist the pleas of so many devout young men who wished to live under his direction, and so he finally emerged from the *Sacro Speco*. With that the second stage of his career had been reached.

Two

Approaching the Goal

Iᴛ ɪs most unlikely that Benedict could at this time
have been deeply read in monastic history. One imagines,
of course, that before he decided to abandon the studies
he had begun in Rome, he would have consulted whatever books he could have found in the libraries there, so
that his impulsiveness was more apparent than real. It is
also possible that while he was stopping at Enfide, he may
have utilized his brief stay in informing himself further
about monastic institutions. But during the three years of
his life in the cave, one must conclude that he had no
books with him or any means of procuring them. What
he gained there was drawn directly from communion
with God, and though nothing can be more valuable,
ordinarily it should be substantiated by the guidance of a
spiritual director, which Benedict did not have, to say
nothing of what he might have learned from the writings
of holy men. The wide reading to which the Rule attests
was done later, when he had leisure and quiet.

What actuated him at this period were two things –
the evident need, brought home to him by the eagerness
of others to learn from him, and his own experience of the
life of an anchorite. It may well have been that he made
use of his three years in the *Sacro Speco* in much the same
way that Ignatius Loyola made use of his period of retire-

ment at Manresa; that is, in the formulation of plans, or at least in the kind of meditation from which a plan gradually evolved. In neither case was the period given up to continuous mystic contemplation – for that is hardly within the power of mortal man. On the other hand, neither Saint sat down saying: 'Let me see; I must draw up a programme.' It was rather that a programme emerged from contemplation, which was the main business of each at the time, though it was not to be the main lifework of either.

It is extraordinary how many disciples had come to Benedict, a very young man who had hidden himself in a well-nigh inaccessible cave. Now that he had emerged, we hear of his establishing at Subiaco a group of twelve monasteries, each under the care of its own abbot but all under his control. Presumably this did not happen all at once, but it was done in a very short space of time, for this was not a long phase in his life. We may say that they mushroomed up rapidly one after the other as soon as it became known what Benedict was doing. He soon found himself at the head of about a hundred and fifty monks – by any standard a large community.

Just how Benedict obtained the land upon which he could build his cluster of cloisters we are not informed. He would hardly have attempted to establish what we call squatters' rights, for these might have been contested at any moment. Therefore, we have to surmise that among the families of Benedict's first disciples were those who would have donated land – land which in that region could have had little monetary value. It is likely that these little abbeys were very simple, consisting of hardly more than an oratory, an open dormitory, a room for reading and storing such books as were obtained, a refectory, and a kitchen. Though some vestiges of these places may still be seen, it is probable that these were remains of later structures and that what Benedict hurriedly built were made mainly of wood; yet of course it must not be forgotten that those rocky hills were so many quarries. We are not told anything about who did the work, but we may assume that, as was certainly true of the later Monte Cassino, the monks themselves were the builders. If so, they would have needed to purchase virtually no materials, and what they needed must have come from donations. Apart from local supporters, it may be supposed that the wealthy men from Rome who brought their sons to Benedict, or well-to-do young men who presented themselves, would have offered fairly substantial gifts, and that the community as a whole remained sufficiently poor. The majority of the first disciples were no doubt humble people who arrived with nothing but a desire to live a more perfect Christian life and could donate only their work.

While it could be that one or two of the shepherds who discovered Benedict when he was still in his cave, and who thought at first that the sheepskin-covered figure was that of a wild beast, joined him, it is more likely that a larger proportion of better-class peasants and artisans did so. Most of these in those times would probably have been illiterate, yet Benedict would hardly have accepted as monks any men incapable of carrying out the provisions of monasticism as envisaged by him. Though we know from the Holy Rule that provision was made for the profession of those who, when making their vows, could not sign their name and had to make a cross on the form of profession – if this was true of Monte Cassino we may take it for granted that it was even more true of Subiaco – we may be sure that from the beginning Benedict accepted only those whom he considered teachable.

He may have been less stringent at the outset in his educational demands, allowing good will and piety to weigh more than anything else – even more than impressive intellectual attainments. But even if it was not absolutely necessary that at the moment of admission a man should be able to read (after all, at Subiaco there could have been few books, even those available for the choir), at least the monks had to be capable of memorizing the Psalter and chanting the psalms with the brethren.

One presumably unlettered monk is mentioned by Gregory the Great but he is not named and merely described as 'a simple, sincere Goth'. The inference to be drawn is that as a barbarian he was illiterate, though one cannot be quite sure. In any event he would have been expected to take his part in the choir, for not until several centuries later did the Benedictines have lay brothers, who were quite unthought of at first. We hear of this man only in connection with one of the Saint's miracles. While the Goth was working with a sickle to clear away the briers at the edge of the lake, its iron blade flew away from the handle and fell into deep water. Upon this the barbarian ran in great distress to Maurus, and Maurus went to tell Benedict about it. (Presumably the utensils and implements the monastery possessed were still so few that this was considered a great loss.) Hearing what had happened, Benedict went down to the lake and thrust the handle of the sickle into the water, whereupon the blade rose at once from the bottom of the lake and reattached itself to the wooden handle. It was characteristic of Benedict to say casually: 'Go on with your work now; there is no need to be upset.' This mild offhandedness marks many of his recorded miracles; it is evident that Benedict did not want to have a repetition of the embarrassing applause that had occurred in the case of the mended sieve at Enfide.

It had been more or less plausibly conjectured that St Benedict wrote a rule for Subiaco that has now disappeared, except for such parts as may have been used in the later codification we know as the Holy Rule. At least we may be sure that the Benedictine family lived from the outset under some regulations, even if these were tentative and depended mainly on the judgment of the abbot. Without them there could have been no orderly life. And we may safely surmise that the regulations that proved their value were retained and the others dropped or modified.

Possibly, too, Benedict was able to secure copies of one or two previous monastic rules and adopted what seemed to him suitable for his purpose. There was, however, no rule available such as he produced, for what then passed as rules were for the most part explanations of what was customary among this or that set of monks, or a set of pious exhortations. Even so, some regulations could have been drawn from these documents that were serviceable, though it must have become more and more apparent that a complete codification would eventually be necessary. But as that could hardly be done without much study – and also the testing of the trial-and-error process – it was impossible to produce at Subiaco the kind of thing Benedict desired. Therefore, it must be supposed that he proceeded according to the mode of other abbots of his time, though with a greater wisdom and moderation. All this could be true even if Abbot Tosti is correct in his surmise that, because in the last chapter of the Holy Rule Benedict uses the expression 'our holy father St Basil' his first monks adopted the Basilian rule as the basis of their way of life. Be that as it may, the Rule as we have it was something that evolved gradually; and the substance of it was practiced long before any of it was written down.

The monasteries of that time were often situated in places where life had many difficulties. At Subiaco, three of the cluster of twelve were at the summit of the rocky height above the lake, and their monks found it very tiring to have to carry every drop of water up a steep and rather dangerous path. Accordingly, they went to Benedict telling him that the only solution they could see was to rebuild elsewhere. Benedict received them with his usual kindness but sent them away with words of encouragement that they may have considered a little empty. But that night he took the boy monk Placid and with him went up to the rocky plateau on which the three monasteries lay. There he prayed a long time and, upon leaving, unobserved by anybody, put three stones together to mark the spot where he had knelt. The next day when the monks went to him again to hear what he had decided, he told them to dig under the stones and they would find water there. Indeed, when they went to the spot they discovered that the stones were already moist and they did not have to dig very deep before they reached a spring which, said St Gregory, 'is still flowing from the top of the mountain into the ravine below'.

This miracle, like that concerning the Goth and his sickle, has a parallel in stories related in the Old Testament. But though there may be those who will suggest that this shows that these miracles are no more than new versions of old stories, and therefore are not to be believed, I cannot see that this follows. Gregory the Great was well aware that there is something very similar in the account of Moses striking the rock in the wilderness or of the prophet who brought an axe head to the surface, and that his readers would also be familiar with those stories. What he (and they) deduced was that the arm of the Lord had not been shortened; that what God had done before He could do again. Obviously one who was merely making up a tale would have been quite capable, unless he had no imagination at all, of inventing miracles of a totally different sort.

Here is another story, this time suggesting the incident of Christ's walking upon the water. One day when Benedict was in his monastery by the lake, Maurus being somewhere near, little Placid had gone out to fetch a pail of water from the stream beyond the dam. He leaned too far over and, being small and having slight strength, was pulled by the current into the water. Benedict by some special insight knew at once of the child's peril and sent Maurus to the rescue. Maurus, promptly obeying, rushed to the edge of the stream where Placid was struggling in the water and, without realizing what he was doing, ran out from the land and pulled him safely back. Afterward there was a charming controversy: Benedict attributed the miracle to the obedience shown by Maurus, whereas Maurus would have it that the miracle was due to the prayers of the Abbot. But Placid settled the matter by saying: 'When I was being drawn out of the water I saw the Abbot's cowl over my head and I judged that it was he who was rescuing me.'

Two interesting facts emerge from the Subiaco experiment – for an experiment was what it turned out to be. Though St Benedict when he composed his Rule showed himself distinctly unfavourable to the idea of a prior (lest that subsuperior should come to regard himself as a second abbot, or even the leader of an opposition party), when the idea of a group of monasteries was given up, the Subiaco plan was preserved to this extent: over each ten monks was appointed a dean. That system has come to be abandoned in favour of monks being appointed to specific offices; the problem of the prior has been solved by the simple method of making the prior always subordinate to the abbot, appointed by him and not by election, and removable at his will.

The second point is that it would seem that in founding these twelve small monasteries St Benedict had in mind something like the modern religious Order under the rule of a general. Congregations of Benedictine abbeys have come to exist, but in our time these leave the individual abbey autonomous. Cluny and Citeaux subsequently attempted a kind of centralization that diverged from the true Benedictine concept, and about this more will be said in a later chapter. It is enough to remark at the moment that if Benedict toyed with the notion of a religious Order, he abandoned it, though he had in fact anticipated what almost every religious Order founded since the thirteenth century has considered as the kernel of its administrative concept. In anticipating at Subiaco what they so carefully aimed at, he turned away, as definitely as from the eremitical plan, from any idea of a group of religious houses under the control of a general.

Just how long Benedict remained at Subiaco is uncertain, but it could only have been a very few years, perhaps two or three but more likely twelve or fifteen. He left because the malicious priest Florentius again appeared upon the scene. As he had failed to poison Benedict and knew that the Saint would be on his guard, he hit upon another device to drive him out. This was to send seven depraved women into the garden of Benedict's monastery, his intention being to strike at the man he hated by

putting his young followers in danger of sin. Some biographers have embellished this a bit by having these
young women dance naked, which of course may have
happened, though St Gregory says no more than that
they were 'depraved'. At any rate this time the malice of
Florentius accomplished its purpose. Benedict waited for
no more save to reorganize the other eleven monasteries
by appointing priors to assist their abbots, for he knew
that Florentius was not concerned with them but only
with getting rid of the man he hated. The monks he left
behind at Subiaco could follow as soon as he had found a
settled abode for them. So accompanied only by the
monks of his own house he set out to find another home.

Benedict had hardly gone ten miles when a message
reached him from Maurus, one of those left behind (one
surmises as one of the newly appointed priors), to say that
they might all now return in perfect safety. It seems that
Florentius was standing on the balcony of his house con-
gratulating himself upon his success when the structure
collapsed and he was killed. Benedict detected a note of
exultation in the message sent by Maurus, but he himself
was filled with sorrow, not only over the dreadful end of
a wicked man but because Maurus had rejoiced. Therefore he showed his displeasure by giving Maurus a heavy
penance, and continued on his way.

There is in this departure from Subiaco an inescapable
inference. After all, the occasion for his leaving having
been removed, Benedict was free to return, now sure of
being unmolested. That he did not return strongly suggests that he was not satisfied with the system of a group
of small monasteries, that even the few years he had spent
there had revealed defects which it is not hard to imagine.
But it was difficult to make a change there, for the terrain

of Subiaco was too broken up into small, steep hills to be
suitable for the erection of one house large enough to
house the many monks who had joined him. As it would
seem that he did not leave immediately after the episode
of the women dancing in the garden – for he first effected
certain administrative changes – he may have had time to
communicate with some of his well-to-do and influential
patrons. It may be that it was through the instrumentality
of the patrician Tertullus that he obtained possession of
the site of Monte Cassino – ever afterward to be associated with his name. Nowhere could he have found a better
place for a large monastery than this extensive plateau
rising so dramatically from the plain. It was removed
from the world but, in its situation on the main road
between Rome and Naples, was a landmark. As such it
was not only admirably suited for the religious life but
almost beckoned to travellers, as the best spot that could
be imagined for dispensing the traditional Benedictine
hospitality.

Three

Monte Cassino

Sᴛ Bᴇɴᴇᴅɪᴄᴛ's transference to Monte Cassino is usually placed somewhere around 530, but Abbot Chapman thinks it occurred ten years earlier, and by then Benedict would have reached at least the age of forty. It seems to me that the earlier date is the more likely, for clearly the move was made because of the troublesome Florentius (though his behaviour may have been the occasion rather than the cause). The incident of the dancing women in the garden, one would think, followed not too distantly behind the attempt on the part of the wicked priest to poison Benedict. From what Gregory the Great tells us, one might infer that the Subiaco experiment lasted only two or three years, which would make Benedict hardly thirty when he departed. But as that, on the face of it, is improbable, I would be inclined to accept Abbot Chapman's chronology, if only because it proposes a date between one that seems too early and another that may be too late.

Clearly Benedict went to Monte Cassino, a place he could never have seen before, because he had a definite reason. It was not like his haphazard settling at Subiaco, for it seems certain that his motive for undertaking a journey that lasted so long as several weeks was that he had obtained a gift of the mountain. Moreover, his

actions on his arrival suggest that he had not only been
given ownership of the place but what might be described
as police rights – all of which points to the donor having
been somebody like Senator Tertullus, a person of political importance.

The road the little group of monks followed struck due
south, through Enfide (unless Benedict took pains to
skirt that place lest he receive renewed adulation) and
then by the Latian Way. Tradition has it that they made
halts at Arcinazzo, Torre, and Alatri, where the abbot,
the Deacon Servandus, was one of Benedict's friends. As
they approached their destination they came upon the
little river Liris, which descends from the mountain. On
its banks was the town of Cassinum, known during the
Middle Ages as San Germano, but now called Cassino
like the height above.

Presumably Benedict and his companions did not lodge
in the town but went straight to the mountain, finding a
cave there, or making a rough shack for shelter. On the
summit was an acropolis which in ancient times had been
occupied by a Roman legion; it was perfectly situated
both as a point that could be strongly held and as a look-
out post over the countryside' Moreover, there was a
sacred wood in which were shrines to Apollo and Jupiter.
St Gregory speaks only of the worship of Apollo, but the
reference in the passage of verse left by Mark the Poet
(not too reliable an authority) also mentions Jupiter.
Here, at least, Mark is borne out by the fact that in 1880 a
stone inscription to this deity was discovered on the
mountain. It is furthermore very likely that the rites of
Mithra were performed there, as this cult was popular for
a while among the Roman soldiers. Finally, it must be
said that the groves were still witnessing the worship of

Venus. It was a large enough place to house comfortably half-a-dozen different shrines.

What is interesting is that this was not all a thing of the past, but that a certain amount of pagan worship was still being practised, for the peasantry in outlying parts was still largely addicted to the ancient gods, despite the legal interdiction. Even fortified by the general prohibition of paganism, Benedict would hardly have ventured to act as he did had he not been given specific authority. At all events the main temple (or shrine) was demolished by the monks and on its site was built the oratory of St John the Baptist, chosen as patron because he was looked upon as the forerunner of monks. This oratory the Abbot Herwegen thinks may have been intended as a chapel for the use of lay people nearby, for the main part of the temple structure was transformed into the monastic church in which the monks could chant their liturgy. In this case the dedication was to St Martin of Tours, the most celebrated monastic predecessor of St Benedict in western Europe. The sacred groves were simply cut down and burned. Every last vestige of paganism was eradicated from the plateau that towered over the district where was to arise the most famous monastery in the Christian world.

Monte Cassino was so perfect a site for the establishment of what Benedict had in mind that one must suppose that it had been described to him in some detail before he went there, and that he did not simply hit upon it by chance. Though this may not have entered his mind at all, that towering landmark could not fail to attract the attention of every traveller on the Via Latina, evoking an inquiry as to what kind of monks lived there. This must have aroused the interest of potential patrons and also attracted men who felt called to the monastic state. It at once dramatically announced its presence and remained withdrawn and secluded.

Benedict had arrived with only a few of the Subiaco monks. They were insufficient in numbers for the extensive work of construction that had to be performed, so we may safely presume the rest of the community farther north was sent for with the least possible delay. Benedict himself was probably the architect, as the monks themselves were certainly the builders. One would at least make this inference about Benedict from what Gregory the Great tells us in Chapter XXII of his *Dialogues*. It seems that when a second monastery was built at Terracina, a seaport thirty miles south-west of Monte Cassino, Benedict promised that he would come and show them where they should build the oratory, the guesthouse, the refectory, and the rest. This he did by appearing to the abbot and prior of Terracina, indicating everything with great particularity. However, as they did not dare put their trust in a mere dream, they put off starting to build until Benedict should arrive in person. As he failed to come, they went back to him and were told that he had already fulfilled his promise and that they should build as they had been instructed.

How good an architect Benedict was is something which we have no means of judging. But that the monks were not always very skilful masons – which is hardly surprising – emerges from the fact that a wall that was being built of stones quarried from the mountain fell upon one of these monk builders and killed him.

About this St Gregory has an interesting story, though some of its details may have to be accepted with a degree of reserve. It seems that while St Benedict was in his room – he had taken for his own cell a small apartment in a tower that rose from the ancient battlements, for they utilized whatever they could of the ancient acropolis – the Devil appeared to him and said jeeringly that he was about to visit the builders. Upon this Benedict, scenting mischief afoot, sent word to the monks to be on their guard, but just as the warning arrived the massive blocks of stone fell. One suspects, however, that Satan did not need to do much pushing but that the wall collapsed because it was not constructed with exact calculation of the perpendicular.

Gregory the Great, as has already been noted, is somewhat given to attributing everything unfortunate that happened to the Devil. Thus he tells us a fearsome story of a stone that the monks could not lift, though they summoned others to their help and though it was in appearance something fairly easy to handle. Therefore, they came to the conclusion that the Devil was sitting on that stone and so sent to Benedict to drive Satan away. The Saint did so, and after he had made the sign of the cross, the stone was lifted with ease. Now Benedict told them to dig under the stone and they reached an idol of bronze which, for the time being, they placed in the kitchen. The result was that the kitchen seemed to be on fire, and that the whole monastery, or as much of it as had been built, was in danger of being burned down. Gregory's comment is: 'Unable to see the fire which appeared so real to his monks [Benedict] quietly bowed his head in prayer and soon had opened their eyes to the foolish mistake they were making.' In spite of this Gregory cannot refrain from adding that the Devil had made them see flames, never even faintly suggesting that the flames perhaps existed only in their excited imagination.

But to return to the young monk who had been crushed

under the falling masonry: Benedict directed that the
mangled body be carried in a blanket to his own cell,
where he had them leave it on a reed mat, after which he
asked everybody to leave. What happened afterward is
not reported, except that Benedict must have prayed hard,
for within the hour the young monk returned to his work
'as sound and healthy as he had been before'. Once more
there are Biblical parallels – that of Elias who raised the
widow's son from the dead, and that of St Peter who did
the same for Tabitha at Joppa.[1] But as I have said, though
these may seem to sceptics to justify a disbelief, which in
any case they would have, they should rather strengthen
belief in St Benedict's miracles. Otherwise we would have
to demand that in order to be accepted every miracle
should be of a completely novel character. This would
only mean in effect that the ingenious concocter of remarkable tales would be more worthy of credence than a sober
chronicler.

This does not mean that I think every miracle that St
Gregory records is to be believed, even though his good
faith is obvious, as it should also be obvious that a man of
his high intelligence and wide experience was not easily
to be imposed on. But I confess myself a little uneasy
about some of the 'diabolical' stories. One suspects that
St Gregory had his mind too full of the text of the psalm,
Dei gentium daemonia. That should be understood in relation to the hideous form of heathenism encountered by
the Jews when they took possession of Palestine. This
really diabolical practice was the sacrifice of children,
'made to pass through the fire'. To the Romans themselves this was shocking, and perhaps the main reason
why the cry that evoked the most intense and immediate

[1] 3 Kings, XVII, 19–24; Acts IX, 40–41.

response was *Carthago delenda est*. It should be remembered that it was from Tyre that these hideous rites had been transplanted to Carthage. Apart from the certain crudities that crept in, the ancient myths of Greece and Rome contain much that is true and beautiful and good. Even the crudities were relatively harmless, because of their domestic character. Of the *lares* and *penates*, the first were only the spirits of one's ancestors and the second the godlets that clustered around almost every human function. It was the nobility of ancient paganism which the Church saluted in the line from the *Dies Irae: Teste David cum Sibylla*. It was, however, paganism in its corrupt decline that was thought of by the Christians of the fifth and sixth centuries. Naturally they were able to regard it only as something horrible, not as an adumbration, however faint, of the better religious faith to come. The gods of the heathen were to them devils.

Yet it may be that the powers of hell in desperation were now doing strange things to prevent the spread of the Christian faith, and resented being ejected from Monte Cassino, one of their last strongholds. So perhaps it really was true that Satan appeared one day to Benedict, not in a dream or disguise but face to face, to make a fierce protest. St Gregory writes that 'his shouts were so loud that the brethren heard him, too, although they were unable to see him'. According to Benedict's own description, the Devil had an appearance utterly revolting to human eyes. He was enveloped in fire, and when he raged against the man of God, flames darted from his eyes and mouth. Everybody could hear what he was saying. First he called Benedict by name. Then, finding that the Saint would not answer, he broke out into abusive language, sneering, 'Benedict, Benedict, blessed Benedict!' from this passing to 'You cursed Benedict! Cursed not blessed! What do you want with me? Why are you tormenting me like this?' In Gregory's Latin the play is on the words *Benedictus* and *maledictus*, but still contains no great sparkle of wit. Yet before we dismiss this incident as a bit of superstition of the Dark Ages, let us recall that in the nineteenth century the Curé of Ars was annoyed by the Devil for twenty years of his life, so that when at last the assaults ceased he was able to say, almost with humorous regret, 'Why, the *grappin* and I had become old comrades!' Benedict got rid of the diabolical pest with more ease and dispatch.

He and his monks settled down to a serene and orderly life, which will be described in greater detail in a later chapter. Though several times threatened during the years of the Gothic War, Monte Cassino never suffered the depredation of violent men until the Lombards destroyed it long after Benedict's death. That, like Subiaco, it was on a mountain, prompted the pleasant distich of the late Middle Ages:

> *Bernardus valles, montes Benedictus amabat,*
> *oppida Franciscus, celebres Dominicus urbes.*

Though only broadly true of these monastic founders, it was the literal truth about Benedict at this time. In his cell in the tower at Monte Cassino, from which he had an even wider sweep of the surrounding country than was obtainable elsewhere, he quietly meditated upon the kind of monasticism he wished to establish. He read much but prayed more, both with the brethren in the oratory, and as he stood in meditation at his open window under the bright and tender Italian sky.

It is this picture of St Benedict we should always keep in mind, this and of the man as revealed by his Rule and of the quiet Benedictine life of recorded history. It might be argued that, more than any other religious founder, Benedict imparted a distinctive spirit to his successors. St Dominic indeed gave his sons a mission – that of preaching; St Francis held up an ideal, which has remained an ideal not only for his friars but for the whole world; St Ignatius with his *Spiritual Exercises* deliberately set out to mould the character of his disciples, and with marked success. But St Benedict, without using any of these methods, or any method at all, but merely providing a Rule – one not intended to be final and fixed but to be interpreted and modified as necessity arose – still deeply permeates the minds of those who follow his monastic method. In fact, it may be said that he has left his mark on every form of religious life, since all are to a greater or less extent based upon the model he provided. And from this point of view it is possible to say that the posthumous part of Benedict's life is the most important part of it.

I stress this point because in the *Dialogues* of Gregory the Great, while we are given a few biographical facts of the ordinary kind, we have what is hardly more than a collection of St Benedict's miracles. These Gregory expressly tells us are by no means all, from which one gathers that he knew of others but omitted them because he had already garnered enough for his purpose, or perhaps because he was not quite satisfied with the substantiation given. For even if Gregory could have known no actual witnesses of the events of Benedict's early years, and therefore wrote down only what was a tradition, we may be sure that he did not record anything unless he was convinced that the tradition was well based.

We may regret that he did not write in the manner of a modern biographer, but in collecting the miracles he took

what interested him and what he believed would interest
his readers. Certainly the form of a dialogue between
himself and his Deacon Peter gives not only grace and
charm and liveliness to what he has presented but offers
an opportunity for explanation and comment. In short,
the stories are not simply planked down but are always
subject to Peter's scrutiny – a circumstance that adds
considerably to credibility.

There are those, as might be expected, who have dismissed the whole collection of stories as being merely
superstitious fables. But this can only be on summary *a
priori* grounds or the basis of a sceptical dogma which is
now rather discredited. No doubt many wonders or
strange happenings are susceptible of a natural explanation, nor is it quite unreasonable for a man, while accepting an undeniable fact, to say that it could be accounted
for were our knowledge of certain mysterious forces
greater than it actually is. But until this hypothesis is
demonstrated (if it ever can be), we are certainly justified
in regarding as miracles happenings that so far as anybody
can see are outside the operation of natural or even preternatural forces. Though considerations of this fine-spun
sort would probably never have crossed St Gregory's
mind, it should at least be remembered that the average of
intelligence was not less then than now, and that Gregory
stood out among his contemporaries. The humorous
shrewdness he exhibits every now and then shows that he
was not easily to be taken in. That he believed in the possibility of miracles does not in the least imply that he gulped
down every marvel he encountered without subjecting it
to the ordinary tests. The safest general judgment would
be that most of what Gregory has written may be confidently accepted, but that it is not incumbent on anybody

to believe every part of it. We should be very uncritical if we threw out the whole of the second book of the *Dialogues* as legendary; at least we should accord it what Abbot McCann calls a 'substantial accuracy'.

Another English abbot, John Chapman, makes a different suggestion, saying that it is frequently assumed that St Benedict's fame was in the main posthumous and rested upon the rapid diffusion of the Rule, though it was rather the other way around: that the reputation Benedict obtained after Gregory had written about him aroused interest in the Rule and helped in its acceptance. That there may be a good deal in this is not unlikely, yet one would prefer to believe that it was the intrinsic merits of the Rule itself that brought this about. It is, however, true that the fame for sanctity that Benedict came to enjoy reposed for the most part on the miracles: people thought he must be very holy because he was so great a thaumaturgist. It is a test that the Church still applies, though not excluding others.

Most of the wonders that have so far been introduced are not easily to be accounted for on 'natural' grounds. This, however, is not the case of those now to be related, for insight or even second sight may be all that was involved and not true prophecy. But in some instances Benedict foretold not merely the event itself but the date when it would occur, as when he informed King Totila that he had only ten years more to live (which would fix their meeting at 542), or when he said that Monte Cassino would be destroyed but that none of the brethren would be harmed. This fell out in 589 just as Benedict had predicted, in the time of the Lombards, but in this case no precise date had been given. Even so, the prophecy was remarkable, but when we are told he read the thoughts of a young monk, the son of a high-ranking official, who was serving him at table and pondering with some surliness, 'Why should I be doing this?' and Benedict instantly reined him in with the reprimand, 'Brother, sign your heart with the sign of the cross. What are you saying? Sign your heart!' – in that instance there may have been something in the young monk's face or eyes that revealed his morose pride.

Much the same could be said of what Gregory tells us of a pious layman who used to visit his brother in the monastery once a year. He made it a practice not to break his fast until he reached the abbey, but on one of his visits he yielded to the persuasion of a companion and did eat. Benedict reproached him with this as soon as he arrived, though why he should have done so is not at all clear, as the man had not committed any sin or broken any rule except the one he had imposed upon himself. But probably no problem of any kind would have been created had Gregory unfolded all the circumstances. If he did not do so, it is likely, as in other cases, that he had no more to impart on the subject. The only comment is that made by the Deacon Peter who said merely: 'This proves that the servant of God possessed the spirit of Eliseus. He, too, was present with one of his followers who was far away.'[1]

A somewhat similar miracle occurred in the case of a man named Zalla, who seems to have been a powerfully placed person under King Totila. It must, however, have been an exaggeration to say that he was so fanatically Arian that 'no cleric or monk could meet him and escape from his hands alive', though no doubt he was a dangerous person to encounter. Zalla was torturing a peasant

---

[1] The reference, of course, is to 4 Kings v, 25–7.

one day to extract his little hoard, when the poor wretch, hoping to escape from his sufferings, said that he had left all that he had in Benedict's keeping. Upon this Zalla led the peasant, his arms bound, to the abbey, where they found Benedict sitting reading at the entrance, and the captive, pointing to the Abbot, said to Zalla, 'There, that's the man I told you about.' Zalla now tried to terrify Benedict by shouting, 'Get up, get up and give back this fellow's property which you have taken.' Benedict made no reply except to raise his eyes from his book and look at the peasant. At once the rope that bound his arms dropped off. It was Zalla who was terrified and who fell at Benedict's feet to beg his pardon. The Abbot, quietly going on with his reading, told some of the monks to take Zalla inside and give him hospitality. Probably the man was so shaken as to need a drink. When he came out a little later, Benedict admonished him not to be so cruel. Zalla left very crestfallen and did not again venture to persecute that peasant.

When Totila appeared at Monte Cassino he also attempted a trick: as he had heard that Benedict possessed the spirit of prophecy, he decided to put the matter to the test. He assigned to a soldier named Riggo the part of impersonating the King, sending the nobles Vultheric, Ruderic, and Blindi, with a bodyguard, to accompany him. But as soon as Benedict saw Riggo he cried, 'Put off those robes, my son, put off those robes; they are not yours.' Riggo was naturally astounded and when the real Totila arrived a little later, Benedict reproved him for his cruelty (which Gregory says resulted in his being less cruel afterward from that time on) and foretold that he would capture Rome (which happened in 542), and that he would die in the tenth year thereafter. This is one of

the very few events which enable us to set down with
certainty a date in Benedict's life.

Others, which do so with less certainty, are the famine
stories. During the ravages of the Gothic War the farmers
fled from their fields, and there were two years during
which this was especially true. Some of these stories, even
when we cannot be too positive as to their date, have
another kind of importance, as showing the kind of a
man Benedict was. For instance, once when the community at Monte Cassino was on the very brink of starva-
tion the Abbot reassured them, telling them to have trust
in God, for all would be well. The next morning thirty
hundredweights of corn were found at the abbey gate, and
no one was ever able to discover who left this corn
there.

Gregory's telling of incidents of this sort gives Peter
the opportunity to ask whether the spirit of prophecy
enlightens prophets constantly or only intermittently. To
this Gregory answers decisively, taking his instances from
the Old Testament, that only now and then is a prophet
able to prophesy. He adds that God by withdrawing this
power from the prophets preserves their humility, for
when the spirit of prophecy does descend upon them they
learn that it comes by God's mercy and what they are at
other times of themselves. It is clear that they were a few
times in his life when Benedict did receive this divine
intimation; but in some of the cases that Gregory adduces
the prophetic power may be no more than intuition or a
knowledge of the human heart.

Another time, when famine was raging in Campania
(this was probably the great famine of 537–8), the stores
of the abbey were exhausted except for a flask of oil. This
a certain Agapitus, a subdeacon (probably not a member

of the community) asked for that he might give it to the poor. Benedict told the cellarer to let Agapitus have this oil, though it was all the abbey had. The cellarer, however, failed to do as he had been told, and Benedict was so angry that he ordered another monk to throw the flask out of the window. This time he was obeyed, but though the glass flask was hurled down a cliff and fell upon rocks it was unbroken and the oil unspilled. At this Benedict ordered it to be given to the subdeacon and in the presence of the whole community rebuked the cellarer for his pride and lack of faith. Such occasional instances show that Benedict could lose his temper or speak with some asperity, though usually he was very controlled and mild. At this time he wished to teach not only the cellarer but all his monks a lesson, and it was one that could not have been lost upon them.

In this story we also see St Benedict's kindness of heart which is also shown in an incident related to Gregory by Benedict's disciple Peregrinus. (The expressions used suggest that Peregrinus had been a monk at Monte Cassino in Benedict's time.) It seems that a man living nearby had fallen into debt and, not knowing what else to do, confided his trouble to the Abbot. He needed what McCann translates as twelve 'shillings', but which was no doubt twelve gold coins of a good deal higher value than that. Benedict was obliged to say that he was sorry but he had nothing to give, but asked the man to come back in a couple of days. On the very day of the latter's return thirteen shillings were found on the top of the cornbin. Benedict gave them all to the harassed debtor, telling him to use twelve to pay his debt and to keep the remaining coin for himself. This last was a charming touch of the Abbot's openhanded generosity: he did not stick to the bare minimum, though it is evident that the abbey could have found a use for the money left over.

Though Gregory the Great declared that he could have recorded many other miracles (and I have made no more than a selection of those he gives), it is evident that Benedict can hardly be considered one of the most notable of thaumaturgists, even if the *Dialogues* present him mainly in that character. Some saints, it should be remembered, have few if any miracles recorded of them. Others, like Francis Xavier, if everything told about him is to be believed, far outdistanced Benedict. As for the fourteenth-century Dominican Vincent Ferrer, we are informed that the demands made upon him for miracles were so great that, in order to have time for his other occupations, he used to ring a bell to let people know when he was free to effect the cures they were seeking. Though one wonders in this case whether a solitary instance has not been represented as a fixed habit, there can be no question about the miracles performed by St Bernard of Clairvaux, when in 1146 he went down the Rhine preaching the Crusade. These were not only extremely numerous but of such a character as to seem incredible were it not that some members of his party kept a joint diary to record the date and place and nature of the miracles performed each day.

Yet it must be said that the greatness of all these saints does not repose so much upon their miracles as upon other facts concerning them: Xavier for his astonishing missionary labours, Vincent Ferrer for his preaching and what he did to end the Great Schism, and Bernard for the sermons which are among the richest expositions of the mystical life. In the case of Benedict, whose Rule is treated somewhat cursorily by Gregory the Great (though as Pope he did much to secure its general acceptance), his primary importance is as the formulator of what came to be the standard monastic legislation. To a modern mind this provides at least as strong a proof of his sanctity as the miracles about him that Gregory collected. However, while the author of the *Dialogues* may have understood this perfectly well, his purpose was to provide the kind of hagiography relished by his age. If he had not produced what may be called this *Fioretti*, we should know virtually nothing about St Benedict except what might be inferred from the Holy Rule itself.

Though they contain not very much more than the miracles, among the most vivid of Gregory the Great's pages are those dealing with Benedict's last months. The reason for this may well be that in regard to this concluding phase of Benedict's life he was able to consult aged monks who could give him first-hand instead of second-hand information, whereas about other matters they could do no more than pass on stories they had heard. Among the most charming of these incidents is the account given of Benedict's last meeting with his sister Scholastica.

Apparently she had first lived the religious life (as so many did at that time) in the house of her parents. But it would seem certain that she had long since moved from distant Nursia to a convent or *cella* near Monte Cassino, as an old lady – especially one who was a nun – would hardly have been able to visit her brother under any other circumstances. In this case it is probable that brother and sister met fairly often, but the meeting described, because it was to be their last, has a special poignancy. And one cannot help feeling that Scholastica had an intimation that death was near. St Philip Neri used to say that such an intimation was commonly given to spiritual people,

c

and we know that he foretold the time of his own death to the very hour.

Benedict and Scholastica met for the last time in a guesthouse not far from the abbey gate, and there they spent the entire day in pious discourse. At the fall of night Benedict told her he must leave her, but she begged him to remain until the morning talking about 'the joys of the heavenly life'. Benedict, however, insisted that he could not stay out of the monastery any longer, upon which Scholastica clasped her hands before her on the table and prayed. Though there had not been a cloud in the sky, by the time she lifted her head the rain was falling in such torrents that Benedict was simply unable to leave. He therefore said reproachfully, 'God Almighty forgive you, sister; what is this that you have done?' She made the characteristic feminine rejoinder, 'I prayed you to stay and you would not hear me; I prayed to Almighty God and He heard me. Now go to the monastery if you can!'

St Gregory offers the comment: 'Contrary to what he had willed, he found a miracle worked by the courage of a woman in the strength of Almighty God. And no wonder if at that time a woman was more powerful than he, considering that she had long desired to see her brother. For according to the saying of St John, "God is charity", and with good reason she was more powerful who loved more.'

It is a delightful and very human story, and Mr T. F. Lindsay makes a further comment along the lines of what Gregory had said: 'Lives of the saints tend to record so much formal perfection that they elicit no more than a formal admiration; yet we are assured that even the greatest of saints shared with us, until the day of their death, the ordinary burden of human weakness and imperfection. I have claimed for St Benedict the quality of common sense, a quality which many people regard, quite simply, as incompatible with "other-worldliness". The story of St Scholastica's tears emphasizes his essential humanity, and thus endears him to us the more.' About the incident and Gregory's own comments Peter the Deacon remarked: 'I find this discussion very enjoyable.' I think that everybody will agree with the good Peter.

Possibly God granted Scholastica's prayer because He knew (even if she did not) that she would never see her brother again in this world. However, Benedict saw her again, in a most unusual way, for three days later, as he stood (as he often did) at the window of his room in the tower, looking up at the sky, he saw a dove entering the courts of heaven. In some unexplained way he understood that this was the soul of Scholastica and that she had just then died. St Gregory continues: 'Overjoyed at her eternal glory, he gave thanks to God in hymns of praise. Then, after informing his brethren of her death, he sent some of them to bring her body to the abbey and bury it in the tomb he had prepared for himself.' Such a vision is by no means unique in the history of the blessed; St Vincent de Paul, for example, knew when St Jane Frances de Chantal died, though she lived at such a distance from Paris that a number of days elapsed before the news could arrive. Her soul, too, he saw ascending to heaven.

Nor was Benedict's vision of the soul of his sister winging to heaven unique with him, for we hear that he saw the soul of St Germanus, the bishop of Capua, being carried heavenward in a ball of fire by angels. This is one of the very few definite dates we have in the life of Benedict, for we know that the bishop died in February, 541. How Benedict knew the one he saw was Germanus

we have no information; indeed, we do not know anything about his ever having met Germanus. Yet, as by
this time Benedict was a well-known personage, and there
are indications that there was a constant stream of visitors
to Monte Cassino, Gregory's silence presents no difficulty.

We do, however, have some corroborative details. At
the time this happened Benedict had staying with him the
Deacon Servandus, abbot of the monastery built by the
patrician Liberius, about twenty miles away. That night
this vision followed another in which the whole world
was gathered into a single ray of light. Benedict, wishing
for someone else to see this, called to Servandus, who
occupied the cell beneath his in the tower, and Servandus
came just in time to see a last glimpse of the kindled sky
before the light faded. Benedict at once instructed a man
known as 'the devout Theoprobus' to go to Cassino and
have a messenger sent that very night to Capua to find
out what had happened to Germanus. When all the details
were learned it was discovered that Germanus had indeed
died at the very hour Benedict had seen the vision.

This would seem to tell against Abbot Chapman's view
that Benedict lived much longer than is commonly supposed, perhaps until 555. For though St Gregory gives
no dates, apparently he arranged his stories about St
Benedict in a chronological sequence as close to the events
as he could. But the death of Germanus is related in the
Dialogues after the death of Scholastica and just before
the death of Benedict himself. One would therefore
gather that even the traditional date of 546 or 547 for the
Saint's death is too late rather than too early. This, however, must not be pressed too far, as King Totila's visit to
Monte Cassino is related in the *Dialogues* twenty chapters
earlier, intervening between miracles that might have

happened at almost any time but two apparently belonging to the famine years of 537–8. As Gregory's chronological guide (if it exists at all) is of a very general kind, I am myself inclined to think that Chapman is not very wide of the mark.

It is a tradition that Benedict died a few days after Scholastica, though this is not stated in the *Dialogues*, where one would surely expect to find recorded so dramatic a fact. There it is merely said that brother and sister were to 'share a common resting-place, just as in life their souls had always been one in God'. This could mean of course, that Benedict died very shortly after Scholastica, and such is the inference commonly drawn from the statement, but it is not inconsonant with the possibility that he outlived her by a dozen years. Be this as it may, as we have no record as to when Scholastica died it casts no light whatever on the date of Benedict's own passing. What Gregory the Great does say is that 'in the year that was to be his last' Benedict foretold the day of his death to a number of his disciples, and to those who were elsewhere (presumably the monks of Terracina) he sent word they would receive a special sign to announce the hour of his death, though we are not informed what this sign was.

St Gregory goes on to say that six days before his death Benedict gave orders for his tomb to be opened, almost immediately afterward being seized with a fever that rapidly wasted his remaining energy. Then, on the sixth day of his illness, he asked his monks to carry him to the oratory, and there he received the Viaticum. After this, rising to his feet, supported in his weakness by the brethren, he stood with his hands lifted up in prayer. So standing and praying, he breathed his last.

That day two monks, one at Monte Cassino, the other

at Terracia,[1] had the same vision. They saw a road covered
with rich carpeting and glittering with thousands of lights,
stretching from the abbey to heaven. And in the brightness
stood a figure of majestic aspect who asked, 'Do you know
who passed this way?' When they said they did not know,
the stranger told them, 'This is the road taken by Benedict, the Lord's beloved, when he went to heaven.' St Gertrude, the Benedictine visionary of the thirteenth century,
declared that St Benedict had appeared to her saying, 'He
who zealously reminds me that I was honoured by the
permission to die standing while at prayer, him will I
faithfully stand by at death.' The posture, it need hardly be
said, is the one normal in the saying of the choral Office.

The remains of the saintly brother and sister were
buried in the same tomb in the chapel of St John the
Baptist, which Benedict had erected on the site of the
ancient shrine to Apollo. The Lombards sacked Monte
Cassino in 589 (though some give 581 as the date) and the
monks fled for refuge to Rome. Until 717 the abbey was
completely deserted, and during that period the bones of
Benedict were translated to the abbey of Fleury in
France about 673, and those of Scholastica to Le Mans.
They had been disovered, after a search of several days
among the ruins of Monte Cassino, by a priest, who
found them buried one on top of the other with a marble
slab between. Having washed the bones, and keeping
them carefully separate, he carried them to France, but
with the utmost secrecy, knowing that this would never
be permitted by the Romans should his deed become
known. In 750 Pope Zachary wrote to the French bishops
asking that the bones be returned to Monte Cassino, and

---

[1] The actual words of the *Dialogues* are: 'one at the monastery, the other some
distance away', but it seems to me the two places named were meant.

he sent a mission to bring them back. Though King Pepin gave support to the Pope's request, there were evasions; however, in the end it would seem that Fleury-sur-Loire (as it was then, though it is now known as Fleury-Saint-Benoît) did give some relics back, and these included some of St Benedict's bones. They were re-buried in a gorgeous tomb at Monte Cassino, but it would seem that only the ashes of St Scholastica are there, her bones having remained at Le Mans. When the Abbey of Monte Cassino was destroyed during World War II, it is worthy of note that the tomb itself was unharmed.

Four

Monasticism before St Benedict

BEFORE COMING to a consideration of the type of monasticism introduced by St Benedict, it would seem desirable to indicate briefly what monasticism was before his day. His Rule was to come to be accepted as the norm throughout western Europe, everywhere supplanting what had gone before it. And yet in what he introduced there was nothing revolutionary, or even anything very novel, though the balance and proportion of his Rule were such as to make it seem something quite new. Still, as Benedict drew freely upon his predecessors – here rejecting and there modifying and everywhere rounding out a code such as had never been attempted before – we shall understand his work properly only if we consider it in relation to what had gone before.

Even during the apostolic age the tendency that was to be systematized as monasticism had shown itself. In those early days obedience, it is true, was only of a general sort – to those in civil or ecclesiastical authority – for there were no monastic superiors in the canonical sense. But even where small groups lived together, somebody had to direct the group. Still, there was nothing that could be called a 'rule', as this was later understood. What are called the 'counsels of perfection' had to serve, instead, though obviously their application called for a definition of the kind only a religious rule could supply.

Celibacy, though strongly recommended by St Paul, was something that could be accepted only by those drawn to it by divine impulsion. Our Lord Himself had said this could not be received by everybody. If it comes to that, we know from St Paul that St Peter (the only apostle he actually names, though he indicates that there were others) took on his missionary journeys 'a sister, a wife'. The priesthood was not celibate until many centuries later, and though celibacy came to be imposed locally in this country or that, it did not generally apply to priests until the time of Hildebrand. Even for some time afterward it would seem that many bishops were obliged to wink at a good deal. A celibate clergy is the result of discipline, and even today most of the Catholic churches of the Eastern Rite in communion with Rome permit marriage prior to the reception of the diaconate – this, of course, only as regards the secular clergy and never those who have bound themselves by a religious rule.

As for poverty, it need hardly be said that not all are called to sell everything they have and give it to the poor, but all Christians should be poor in spirit and, when they retain their wealth, use it for God's glory. Our Lord again is the source of this counsel, for He uttered the most serious warnings about the extreme peril of riches to the soul. As for St James, he fiercely cries, 'Go to now, ye rich men, weep and howl for your miseries that shall come upon you!' Though the continuation of the passage we have cited indicates that he was thinking of the injustices perpetrated by the rich (and in his day at least it was all but impossible to be rich except by such means), it is also quite clear that poverty was his ideal. It remains the ideal of all those who remember the poverty of Christ and His Mother.

The early and unorganized practitioners of the counsels of perfection, even when they lived together in groups, had no monastic dress, nothing to distinguish them from other people except their sobriety of behaviour and, as time went on, their asceticism. We do not, in fact, hear much about asceticism (in the sense in which the word is commonly understood) until the mass flight from the wicked centres of population into the desert during the fourth century. It was really part of a shocked recoil from the world, though also a means of overcoming evil propensities in oneself, and in the East one cannot but think that it contained some tinge of oriental pessimism.

This asceticism has been greatly exaggerated and has given the early monks a rather bad name among many people of today. But it should also be said that if it was of a very extreme sort in some instances, the tendency of monasticism, when it came to be something like a system, was to restrain it. At the same time, as the early monastic movement was so highly individualistic, it left each hermit pretty much to his own devices. Still, for the most part, the austerities were at first what Abbot Butler calls, in his *Lausiac History of Palladius*, natural rather than artificial. That is to say monks went in for prolonged fasts;[1] they deprived themselves, to the very limits of what they could endure, of sleep; they exposed themselves to heat and cold; and they maintained an all-but-unbroken silence. They did not, however, often scourge themselves, and their clothing, while frequently merely the skins of

[1] A certain amount of carefully regulated fasting and abstinence has, of course, long been part of the settled law of the Church. The reference here, however, is to ordinary fasting.

animals and as such very uncomfortable, did not involve the hair shirts that later ascetics (even the charming and gay Sir Thomas More) were wont to adopt. Nor did the ascetics of the Desert wear the spikes or spiked chaplets, such as were used by St Rose of Lima as late as the seventeenth century.

We hear that by 325 there were more than 5,000 of such solitaries, women as well as men. They worked fairly hard, despite a life that one would suppose could have left them little energy for work, but it was almost always an occupation of a kind that would not interfere with their contemplation: the raising of vegetables for their sustenance, or the weaving of mats and baskets from the reeds they cut at the river edge. Usually some of these were sold to purchase food, but cases are known where the solitary lived too far from any settled habitation to make it worth his while to travel to it with his wares, and after the mats and baskets he made had become a great mound he simply burned them – after which he would begin all over again. In fact, most of this work was done merely to give those in the Desert something to occupy them, to prevent sloth from overtaking them, although it no doubt also helped to preserve their balance; perhaps even their sanity.

These hermitages were scattered, some of the solitaries living absolutely alone, others with one or two companions. The hermits never met as a body except in church on Saturday and Sunday; and though there was no superior in the true monastic sense, the elders exercised some guidance – it was purely voluntary as to whether or not this was followed. That such guidance was wise appears from the recorded sayings of the Fathers. Even the rigorous St Anthony remarked: 'There be some who wear out their bodies with abstinence: but because they

have no discretion, they be a great way from God.' Such
things make it evident that some effort was made to keep
ill-advised enthusiasts within the bounds of moderation.

That this was necessary in the case of the injudicious
young is made all the more apparent from what Helen
Waddell in her *Desert Fathers* summarizes of the account
left by Palladius of the famous Macarius and of the way
he was for a while animated by an unlovely competitive
spirit: 'Did he hear that one Father ate only a pound of
bread, himself was content to nibble a handful of crusts;
did another eat no cooked food for the forty days of
Lent, raw herbs became his diet for seven years.' More
than that, learning of the austerities practised at the
monastery of Pachomius, Macarius journeyed there in disguise, and, though admitted, was kindly told by the abbot
that of course it would not be expected of an old man,
not used to such abstinence, to equal the younger and
stronger brethren. Of these one fasted until vespers,
another for two days, another for five, and still another
stood up all night and then sat weaving his mats all day.
Upon hearing this, Macarius determined to outdo them
all. Therefore, providing himself with plenty of fibres for
plaiting, he stood in a corner for the whole of Lent, eating
nothing, drinking nothing, and never lying down or
kneeling or speaking, though – to avoid seeming to be
ostentatious! – he would partake of a few raw cabbage
leaves on Sundays. This made the rest of the monks (for
Pachomius had established the first institution that may
be called a monastery) so furious that they went in a body
to their abbot demanding that unless this creature who
was bringing them all into contempt left, they would all do
so, and that very day. Faced with such an ultimatum,
Pachomius meditated and prayed, whereupon it suddenly

dawned upon him who this austere old man was. 'He went to find him, led him by the hand to his private oratory, and there kissed and greeted him by name, gently reproaching him for his efforts at disguise from one who had for many years desired to see him. "I gave thee thanks that thou has clouted the ears of these youngsters of mine, and put the conceit out of them. Now, therefore, return to the place from whence thou camest; we have all been sufficiently edified by thee: and pray for us." '

In the same way the Abbot Anthony used to say: 'Who sits in solitude and is quiet hath escaped from three wars: hearing, speaking, seeing: yet against one thing shall he continually battle: that is, his own heart.' Another abbot, Isidore, when asked why the devils feared him so much, made answer: 'From the time I was made a monk, I have striven not to suffer anger to mount as far as my throat.' Similarly the Abbot Silvanus said: 'Never have I suffered to remain in my heart a thought that angered me.' And in the anonymous *Sayings of the Fathers* we find a charming story which, like so much else there, should be remembered instead of the fantastic mortifications recorded of some of the monks of the Desert. 'There were two old men living together in one cell, and never had there risen even the paltriest contention between them. So the one said to the other, "Let us have one quarrel the way other men do." But the other said, "I do not know how one makes a quarrel." The first said, "Look, I have set a tile between us and say, 'That is mine', and do thou say, 'It is not thine, it is mine.' " So as in this way contentions arise, they set a tile between them, and the first one said, "That is mine," and the second made reply, "I hope it is mine." And the first said, "It is not thine: it is mine." To which the second could only say, "If it is thine, take it."

After which they could find no way of quarrelling.'

Almost simultaneously with St Anthony's establishment of an organized eremitical life in northern Egypt,
St Pachomius established farther south a cenobitical type
of monasticism. Though he provided his followers with
a rule, it sought only to fix a fairly moderate level of
observance, then left the individual monk to add to his
austerities according to his zeal and courage and strength,
but encouraging him to do so. Even if this still gave too
much rein to the spirit of competition (we now find
monks working together in the fields and plying all kinds
of trades), a communal spirit was fostered, which was all
to the good. However, there were as yet no vows, except
those that the individual may have taken privately, nor
was there any religious habit in the modern sense. It was
considered that once a man had entered the monastic or
eremitical life he was committed to it until death.

If the Desert was stony and sandy, the life of the monk
and hermit grew even more stringent when their main
centre shifted, as it did a little later, to Palestine and
Syria. Now the bodily austerities that were to some extent
controlled in Egypt were sometimes savagely emphasized.
We therefore encounter 'pillar solitaries' of whom St
Simon Stylites is a type, and others whose performances
were equally severe and arduous. It is hard to know
how such people were even able to chant the Psalter, unless they knew it all by heart and said it to themselves;
still less could they have assisted at Mass or received the
sacraments. It all seems very far removed not only from
monasticism as we know it but from ordinary Christian
living. The Desert had been a good deal better than that.
Yet we must remember that Benedict himself in his youth
spent three years in a cave at Subiaco, and though he may

have taken a Psalter with him (for at that time he could hardly have known all the psalms by heart), he evidently did not feel obligated to attend the services in any church. However, we should also remember that he decisively turned away from that sort of individualism when he gathered his disciples into a community.

But to go back to the history of pre-Benedictine monastic development. St Basil, after a visit to Egypt, Palestine, and Syria, made a further advance along the lines of cenobitic order, moderating even more than Pachomius. With Basil there was a common habitation, a refectory with meals at set hours, and a daily Office, if perhaps not daily Mass. Basil's importance was not merely that he introduced a rule binding upon all, but that for the first time he declared definitely in favour of the cenobitical life as against the eremitical. Pachomius, while pointing in that direction, had attempted (as did others later) to combine the two modes. In fact, he permitted so much individualism that extravagance was often incited. Moreover, he went beyond the first Benedictine monks in the sense of conceiving the serving of hospitals and schools and orphanages. Though Benedictines in due course came to do these things, too – and on a scale that St Basil had never envisaged – St Benedict started his career by confining activities strictly to the monastery, building up within its cloister the life he saw to be most necessary. But his Rule was sufficiently elastic to be in consonance with subsequent extensions.

There were many other monastic experiments, St Augustine, for example, trying to organize his diocese upon that plan, though what is called the 'Rule of St Augustine', and followed in its general principles by a number of religious orders, was not a rule in the Bene-

dictine sense. But monasticism of a severe type found its
way into Gaul, and we hear of St Athanasius bringing
with him a Nitrian monk to Italy as early as 339. Certainly Benedict had known from his youth of both the
cenobitic and eremitical type in his native country, but
we have seen his first contacts with them were far from
being fortunate, and one would gather the same thing
from what he has to say in his Rule.

Things were better in the monastery established by St
Martin of Tours at Ligugé, as in the other he founded at
Marmoutier, but in them, as at the famous monastery of
Lérins, the island just off Cannes, and at Marseilles, where
John Cassian composed his *Institutes* and *Collations*, the
discipline, though admirable, was excessively austere,
being in many ways a reversion to the Desert. These
Gallic monasteries became great nurseries for bishoprics,
and their rules, incomplete though they were, provided a
source upon which Benedict was to draw freely, though
he kept Basil as his main guide. Moreover, St Basil had
already introduced a good deal of moderation, thus
paving the way for the further moderation of St Benedict.

As for Irish monasticism, though we know that it appeared very early, not much that is definite is known. We
also know that it was introduced into Wales by Irish
missionaries, and that St David patterned his life upon
that of the Egyptian monks. Much the same is true of the
monasteries founded by the Irishman St Columbanus at
Luxeuil, St Gall, and Bobbio. These Irish monasteries
were notable centres of learning, preparing the ground
for the reconstruction of Europe, and also it may be said
for the mission of Benedict. It is to be remarked that the
monks of St Columbanus, who was born about the time
that St Benedict died, became leading propagators of the

Benedictine monastic concept, though at first combining only some features of his Rule with their original practices and customs.

It is safe to assume that about this time there were monks and hermits in Spain, but nothing whatever is known about them. We can only surmise that they derived their inspiration from the Desert. It therefore had no bearing upon the mode of monasticism to be developed by Benedict. In any event, our main concern must be with monasticism as it had appeared in Italy, for only later could Benedict have informed himself about the general history of the institution elsewhere and derived what hints he felt he could use from the rules left by his predecessors.

The prevailing ideas were somewhat confused. We know that there was a tonsure, somewhat larger in the case of monks than in that of ordinary priests, habiliments that marked the monk and hermit as different from other men but still not a religious habit, as we understand the term, and no vows, except that the wearing of the *melota* bound under a rigorous obligation. All was rather capricious and unorganized, in one place existing great austerity, in another a laxity and unruliness so great that monks were such in hardly more than name. Abbot Herwegen's description of the situation is: 'In Italy monachism was understood to be a collection of ascetic prescriptions and of traditional customs and forms. In the slavish imitations of Oriental cloister life, which was at that time general in the West, lay the proximate danger of external observance without the spirit that should animate it. Hand in hand with this went an unchecked individualism, which could easily dispense with a superior, and which saw in the abbot only a functionary who according to the tradition belonged to the exterior realization of the monastic ideal.' Here and there a particular abbot, because of his personal holiness or force of character, might have a good deal of influence during his lifetime, and then after his death his successor, unable to exert control, would see his community slip rapidly into great laxity.

St Benedict quite early in his life must have come to perceive the condition into which the monastic institute had fallen. When he came to write the Holy Rule, in the very first chapter, after indicating that there could be admirable hermits as well as admirable monks but giving his own verdict in favour of the cenobitic manner of life, he states that there were two other kinds of monks that were not admirable at all. One class was that of the *sarabaites*, 'who not having been tested, as gold in the furnace, by any rule or the lessons of experience, are as soft and yielding as lead'. These were monks only in name, for they lived by twos and threes, or even singly, doing whatever they chose to do, but calling it holy because they did it. Of these Benedict says sternly, 'Their tonsure marks them as liars before God.' Still worse, if possible, were the so-called monks of another kind, those he terms *gyrovagues*, who went wandering about from monastery to monastery, 'ever roaming and never stable, given up to their own wills and the allurements of gluttony, and worse in all respects than the *sarabaites*.' By this time he must have had a considerable experience of these people, if only as casual and not very edifying guests in his own abbey. He concludes: 'Of the wretched life of all these folks it is better to be silent than to speak.'

Walter Dirks says in a book written in a rather cloudy German manner, though it is clear on this point: 'St Benedict of Nursia had other thoughts and feelings on this subject. It is not only moderation, community, law – the Roman style – that distinguished his foundation from the hermitages and monastic republics of Egypt. It is not only the West that contrasted in his foundation with Eastern monasticism; in him a new relationship to society and to history was proclaimed. He served not only the Church and her history, but also society and its history. In him the unity of redemptive history, as the indivisible history of mankind, became clear in a new fashion.' In other words, monasticism is not properly understood if it is regarded as an isolated phenomenon, but only in its relation to all human activities.

The stability, which was one of the vows taken by Benedictine monks, was undoubtedly originally forced on Benedict as an absolute necessity by what he had observed of the *gyrovagues*, the wandering monks of whom he speaks with such scorn. It should be remembered that the whole of Europe was undergoing the throes of the Great Migrations. It was at a time when nothing was stable, when most people were either uprooted, or were likely to be, that Benedict perceived the necessity of providing a fixed centre. Though this could be only for his monks, it did a great deal to calm the upheavals of the times. As Dirks says: '*Stabilitas loci* meant the end of the Great Migrations. The period we call by that name still continued, but here, for the first time it was told to stop, not in any polemical way but in accordance with the law and the method of the saints who do not talk but do and are. The Benedictine existence was the end of the Great Migrations.'

Five

The Holy Rule

THE DATE of the Rule composed by St Benedict, like so many of the things about him, is a matter of uncertainty. Abbot Chapman argues that it was composed at the instance of Pope Hormisdas, who reigned from 514 to 526. This might place its publication after the end of that period, for even had it been begun at the prompting of Hormisdas (and even that much is conjectural), it might not have been completed until several years after the Pope's death. Abbot McCann will have none of this, and he probably is right, for he points out, and Dom Morin and Abbot Butler agree, that the borrowings from Benedict which Chapman fancied he had traced in the Rule of St Caesarius of Arles (probably written in 534) are more likely to be borrowings on Benedict's part from Caesarius. If so, the Rule was not much earlier than 540, though of course parts of it might go back to Benedict's years at Subiaco. But we may be morally certain that though the Holy Rule as we have it is less than 20,000 words in length, it was not a work produced at white heat in a few weeks but a slow distillation spread over several years. Such things are the result of careful consideration and frequent revision.

As for the question as to why it was written and for whom, it is possible to be a little more definite. Primarily it was written for Monte Cassino and for the guidance of the abbot who would take the place of Benedict, who was now growing old. It may also have been intended for the monastery he had founded about this time at Terracina, a town on the west coast only slightly south of the main abbey. And it may well be that other abbots of the time asked Benedict to draw up a rule, for they must have realized their lack of just such systematizations as he formulated. Though they need not have adopted every detail in his work, they would assuredly have found it useful, even when they combined it with some other rule or rules. As for Pope Hormisdas, while he may have suggested such a work to Benedict, neither he nor his successors made any attempt to impose the Benedictine Rule generally. It made its way solely on its merits, and these were only gradually generally recognized. Even St Gregory the Great, though he is often considered almost the co-founder of Benedictinism, never seems to have exercised any pressure in this regard despite the fact that as Pope he was in a position to do so. This may be partly because the monastic institution as such was exempt from episcopal control. But even in his *Dialogues* Gregory has little to say about the Rule.

The original manuscript was preserved for a considerable time at Monte Cassino but eventually was lost in a fire. The oldest extant copy of the Rule is that made at the beginning of the eighth century by the Benedictine monks at Canterbury, and is now at the Bodleian Library at Oxford. The best manuscript, however, is the one made at Aachen about a hundred years later. Though now and then one may detect a tendency on the part of scribes to elaborate – for according to later standards (as also earlier ones) Benedict may be considered too unadorned

in style – the patient labour of scholars has now managed
to reach with substantial accuracy a reproduction of the
text as it came from his hands. Dom Linderbauer's critical
text of 1928 with its full apparatus is generally acknowledged to be the best edition in this respect, but that by
Abbot Butler, the *Editio Critico-practica*, first published in
1912, though it strives to remove some of the peculiarities
of the Saint's Latin, is considered the best for ordinary
purposes. I have used neither, but the Holy Rule as given
paragraph by paragraph, with Latin and English in
parallel columns, in the large commentary made by the
Abbot Delatte, but consulting sometimes for convenience
an English translation, devoid of all notes, issued by St
John's Abbey of Collegeville, Minnesota, and Abbot
McCann's version in Latin and English, the most recent
edition of all. My purpose in this little book extends no further than the presentation of a few of the more salient facts.

St Benedict's use of the *lingua vulgaria* is, as Abbot
Butler has pointed out, no proof that he did not know the
Latin used by cultivated people; it merely indicates that,
being a very practical person, 'he automatically wrote his
Rule in the dialect spoken in daily life'. This kind of Latin
has very real merits of its own, even if it is not in the
'classical' vein. Cardinal Bembo, the famous humanist of
the sixteenth century, made himself slightly ridiculous by
saying that the Vulgate was too barbarous for a man of his
exquisite sensibilities to read. The impossible effort made
by such people to return to Cicero was what, more than
anything else, made the popular Latin of the Middle
Ages a dead language. St Benedict, so far from being a
clumsy writer, is vivid and intensely personal, though
Mr Lindsay thinks his Latin betrays 'an imperfect education, supplemented by later study'. His frequent epigrams,

however, prove the Rule to be 'the composition of an artist, carrying us deep into the heart of the author'.

There are those who, discovering that St Benedict has drawn from a vast number of different sources, sometimes using them almost unchanged, have tended to think of his Holy Rule as a mere compilation. Nothing could be a more complete misjudgment of the matter; the wonder is the way Benedict transforms all that he touches, so that his work, taken as a whole, is seen to be decidedly original and personal. He draws freely upon Cassian, the learned Abbot of Marseilles, St Basil (and to such an extent that one theory is that the Rule of St Basil was followed during Subiaco days), St Jerome, St Augustine, Leo the Great, the *Vitæ Patrum*, the Fathers, and most of all the Scriptures. Indeed Abbot Butler in his second edition of the Rule lists no less than three hundred and forty-six quotations (or at least allusions) in the work, though some of these may have been no more than accidental similarities, along with echoes from such heathen writers as Sallust and Terence. Yet upon all this highly disparate material Benedict has stamped his personality so successfully (though no doubt quite unconsciously) as to make everything his own. In many ways one gets to know him, at any rate as a man, almost better through the Holy Rule than through the *Dialogues* of St Gregory.

A second criticism of the Rule is that it is nothing but a legal code, the suggestion being that it is as colourless as a code. That it is a legal code is of course true, and Abbot Chapman even enumerates a large number of the legal terms employed. But colourless it is not, unless the reader be very superficial and unsympathetic. The tone throughout is one of fatherly solicitude, and while occasional sternness appears, that, too, is fatherly, for the monks, being the sons of the abbot – whose very title is derived from the Syriac word meaning father – sometimes need his correction. The very first words of the Prologue (though this, like the preface of a book, might have been written last) are: 'Hearken, O my son, to the precept of your master, and incline the ear of your heart: willingly receive and faithfully fulfil the admonition of your loving father, that you may return by obedience to Him from whom you had departed by the sloth of disobedience.' A gentle and paternal note is struck at once.

The Rule appears to be somewhat confused in its arrangement, suggesting that it was not coldly planned but rather that topics were treated as they occurred to Benedict. Broadly the divisions are, first, persons, dealing with the abbot, his monks, children, and old men, and the special consideration that had to be given in such cases; the sick, guests, novices, and those who are engaged in various handicrafts; these, however, do not come in regular sequence but are scattered in various chapters throughout the document. Next come the 'officials of the monastery': the prior, the cellarer, the cooks, the readers at table, the novice-master, and so forth. Then Benedict treats the 'monastic virtues' in a number of chapters, the most important of which are those on 'Obedience', and 'The Instruments of Good Works' – the latter a very long chapter, which is hardly more than a compendium of various Christian virtues, not all of which are peculiar to monks, but specially stressing humility, poverty, work, and silence. The Divine Office is treated in Chapters VIII–XX and again in Chapters XLII and XLVII. Finally there are disciplinary regulations, though these are also scattered here and there throughout the Rule.

The last seven chapters have been taken by some as a

supplement to the Rule, and they may be right, though it does not matter a great deal if it is so, except as this may throw further light upon St Benedict's method of composition. The main point is not the apparent lack of symmetry, but the underlying unity of the Rule when taken, as it should be, as a whole. It would have been a very simple matter for Benedict to have transferred the conclusion of Chapter LXV to Chapter LXXIII. That he failed to do this would indicate that it was a matter of indifference to him as to just where it came. The words are: 'And, especially, let him observe this present Rule in all things; so that, having ministered well, he may hear of the Lord what that good servant heard, who gave wheat to his fellow servants in due season: "Amen, I say unto you, he shall place him over all his goods."' As that winds up the last of the chapters on the Abbot, one might have expected it to come at the very end of the Rule; as it does not, it becomes evident that Benedict did not greatly care in what precise place he said a thing, all that mattered was that it should be said. This was all the less important because some part of the Rule was read aloud every day, so that every monk soon got it all by heart.

St Benedict loses no time in explaining that he intended to impose nothing harsh on those who followed his Rule, in fact, he is at times almost apologetic on this score. He must be admitted to be much more moderate than most of his predecessors, but his wisdom has proved its value through the centuries. Though anybody who obeys his injunctions will find them strict enough, Benedict is aware of human failings and weaknesses and always shows an indulgence toward those who, on account of tender years or advanced age, need some mitigation. Throughout he is kind and reasonable and offers his Rule with

characteristic modesty as merely intended 'for beginners'
– and this would seem to indicate that he considers the
hermit, such as he himself had been in his youth, as having
reached a more advanced stage in the spiritual life. Yet
very few Benedictines have left the cloister in search of
that higher degree of perfection, if such it really be. Benedict himself says that of all the various kinds of monks
the cenobites were the 'strongest'; it is only for these, he
says, that he designed his Rule, a statement that carries all
the more weight because of his personal experience.

It must nevertheless be said that there have been
through the ages a handful of men who permissibly have
left an abbey governed by his Rule for another, either
where the Rule is given a very strict interpretation (as
among the Trappists) or to the Carthusians who, though
living in community, constitute a semi-eremitical Order.
According to canon law anybody is free to proceed from
the lower to the higher; only those who wish to reverse
the process have to obtain special permission from the
Holy See. It is worth noting that the Carthusians, when
they were recently introduced into the United States, had
as their American founder a former Benedictine who for
many years was a professor at the Catholic University of
America in Washington, D.C., where he also practised as
a psychiatrist (being a doctor of medicine as well as a
doctor of philosophy) and had established a school for
retarded girls.

This brings me to the question of whether the Benedictines live according to the contemplative or the active
mode of life. Abbot McCann, when asked whether the
Rule is a mystical or ascetical document, answers without hesitation that it is ascetic, even if its asceticism is
of a very moderate sort. But as to whether the Rule pro-

poses an active or contemplative life, he says 'that is a more difficult question and will need a longer answer'. His solution is that the Benedictine life allows for and promotes contemplation, but provides for it in the Divine Office, private prayer, study, silence, and work, the goal of which is the perfect love of God. Yet one can hardly say of the Benedictines, as St Thomas Aquinas said of the Dominicans (or not in quite the same sense), that they seek to combine contemplation with activity, that their object is *tradere aliis contemplata*, or to make available to others the fruits of contemplation. The Benedictine, though he may engage in various forms of active work – which in fact he often does – is not committed by the Rule to any kind of work at all, except what he performs in the monastery. Here St Benedict envisaged manual work, though from the beginning circumstances obliged some to substitute the copying of books, or handicrafts, or even the production of works of art, and in our times few monks except lay brothers do physical work, the rest being engaged in teaching or preaching or even the writing of books.

If we look at the question more broadly (or perhaps it is more narrowly), during his life on earth a hermit can hardly spend all his time in contemplation, though undoubtedly there are forms of monasticism that further contemplation more directly than does the Benedictine. As Abbot Butler remarks, 'Judged by Egyptian standards [even] Trappist life is not contemplative,' for the simple reason that Trappists do a good deal of manual work today, much more than is usual among other Benedictines. Yet St Thomas expressed the tradition of his time in saying, 'The religion of monks is instituted for the contemplative life.' One has to fall back upon the idea that, in so far as the Benedictine is to be considered a contemplative, it is within the framework of his primary function, the solemn choral recital of the Divine Office, the *Opus Dei*, 'to which nothing is to be preferred'. As St Gregory the Great wrote in his *Morals*: 'Christ set forth in Himself patterns of both lives, that is the active and contemplative united together.' And Gregory, though as Pope he became immersed in administrative details, was one of the great early exponents of the mystical life. Therefore it would seem that the common distinction, though it has validity, does not necessarily involve a separation of the two modes.

As for asceticism, while the Benedictine Rule certainly assumes it, it also seeks a moderation that would prevent all extravagance and singularity. In the Desert individualism often obtained full rein, and Desert standards for a while largely governed the monastic standards of the West, at least in certain localities. But though it must not be said that St Benedict did not demand a certain austerity from his monks, he modified even the modification that St Basil had incorporated in his Rule. Benedict does not say that none of his monks may go beyond the minimum requirements that he lays down, but he is very clear and emphatic that, even during Lent when some additional asceticism is very much in order, nothing must be done without the express permission of the abbot himself. This is to guard against anything like the rivalry in ascetic practices that appeared in the Desert; St Benedict knew that such things, even when they are commendable in themselves, are liable to engender pride, than which there is nothing more dangerous to the soul. So he thinks that ordinarily it will be quite enough if the Rule be observed faithfully; its mortifications are interior rather than exterior. In this respect he foreshadows asceticism as understood today, or even since the time of St Francis de Sales. That saint, by the way, when asked by a nun what she should do to attain perfection (evidently she was expecting him to name some special mortifications) got the answer that for her the best way was to close doors quietly. One must suppose that her habit of slamming them imposed a quite needless mortification upon the community in which she lived.

Some things in the Rule are guiding principles rather than specific regulations. For instance, in the chapter, 'The Instruments of Good Works', Number 21, 'To prefer nothing to the love of Christ', or 31, 'To love one's enemies', or 32, 'Not to render cursing for cursing, but rather blessing', and 33, 'To bear persecution for justice' sake' – these fall under the injunctions to be remembered by all Christians and not only by monks. So also with many other things in this chapter. But the Abbot Delatte rightly points out that these sayings are the 'tools, implements, resources' of the Christian life, that it seems to us to make virtue easier when expressed in 'a short, pithy, and well-turned phrase, which in its very perfection has a gracious charm', and that Benedict does lay considerable stress upon the faults most common among religious, 'whether by aversion or detraction'. Again in the long chapter on humility – and apart even from what is said there, humility is inculcated as the virtue essential to the monk – we have something which in the very nature of things is secret, which the humble would be the very last of all people to claim, or even to recognize in themselves. It is true that it may be possible for a while to make a parade of humility, but, as in the obnoxious case of Uriah Heep, the pretence is certain sooner or later to be discovered. The twelfth degree of that virtue as expounded by Benedict (he here follows John Cassian) is when the monk shows humility in his posture, his gestures, the expression of his face – though this, too, might for a while be more or less successfully carried off by a hypocrite. Yet Benedict stresses it as lying at the very heart of the monastic life.

Details about the Rule (though no attempt can be made here to discuss them all) will have to be left to subsequent chapters. What must be said at this place, because it is fundamental, is that Benedict never thought of himself as founding an 'Order', unless he toyed with this idea at the time he established his group of twelve monasteries at Subiaco. The very fact that he did not do so shows that he turned away from the idea of an Order to a very different concept. It is now customary to speak of the 'Benedictine Order' and what St Benedict instituted has come to be regarded as a religious Order by canon law. But Benedict's idea was that each abbey was to be completely autonomous; even when a number of abbeys grouped themselves for convenience into a congregation, autonomy remained, leaving it possible for each abbey (or abbot) to modify according to circumstances, as has, in fact, occurred, although all true Benedictines are guided by the original principles of their founder.

It is still possible, even admitting the necessary distinctions made by canon law, to look upon each separate Benedictine abbey today as constituting a religious Order in itself. There is among Benedictines no such person as a general, and while Leo XIII probably had it in mind that a general would eventuate from his creation of an Abbot Primate operating in Rome as a centre, the other Benedictine abbots have managed matters in such a way that the Primate has his hands so full of other obligations as to have no time to attempt (even should he wish it) the enlargement of his office. Yet as Abbot Butler has pointed out, human nature being what it is, one may expect a Primate to appear one day who, in his ambition, will attempt to widen the scope of his present limited authority and make himself a general, in the usual meaning of that term. So far, however, this has not happened, and one may hope that the traditions of the primacy have already had time to take a form clear and strong enough to prevent its ever happening. Anything else would change the whole character of Benedictine life.

It there is no Benedictine general, it follows that there are no provincials who are governed by him. Instead, there are merely abbots, and while each abbot may have a number of dependencies – priories or parishes – under him, yet each governs no more than these. It is into the individual abbey the monk enters and for it that he is professed, not for any 'Order' or province. Though it is possible for a monk to leave the abbey to which he is attached and to become affiliated with another, this does not in the least affect the rule of stability, for the transference can be made only by permission, and this will not be given except for a compelling reason. Neither can he be transferred at the will of his abbot, except from the abbey of his profession to one of its dependent houses.

It will be seen that all this is quite different from the Orders that arose in the thirteenth century and later. To carry out their work the Dominicans and Franciscans, for example, had to obtain a mobility that the Benedictines lacked, and their emergence was providential, for new conditions in society demanded that new concepts of the religious life be admitted. One may go further and say

that, while the various orders of friars retained the ancient
tradition of monasticism to the extent of making the
choral saying of the Divine Office incumbent on all
except lay brothers, the Jesuits and other societies and
congregations of what are called 'clerks regular' that have
appeared from the sixteenth century on have managed to
free themselves even from the choir, though one of the
Popes for a short while insisted upon the Jesuits saying
the choral Office. One might add that the word 'Benedictine' was not for some time attached to those who
followed the Holy Rule; when it came to be used it was
mainly as a means of distinguishing monks of this sort
from the new Orders beginning to arise.

Yet invaluable as is the work that has been done by the
friars and clerks regular, and which they could effectually
carry out only by adopting a new mode of the religious
life, the monks who observe the Holy Rule continue to
show that they have a place in the modern world, that,
in fact, they are needed more than ever. The Benedictines
continue to provide a fixed point and have provided a
Rule from which other Orders could select whatever
fitted in with their special needs. Thus the Oratorians
have gone directly to Benedict for their concept of the
autonomy of the individual house. Those Orders that say
the Office in choir, as the older ones still do, at least in
this respect resemble Benedictines. All of them – even
those who like the Sulpicians and Paulists, are only
groups of priests living in community but unbound by
vows – derive the idea of the novitiate from the Holy
Rule, for there it first appeared. Finally it might be said
that the idea itself of religious vows, whether simple or
solemn and perpetual, comes from the same source,
though now it is a matter upon which the Church care-

fully legislates. In short, what may be described as 'Benedictinism' (an ugly word suggesting a degree of systematization never in the mind of the Saint) must still be
regarded as in some sense the concept to which everything
was referred, even when it was modified or definitely
departed from. For many centuries it was accepted everywhere in western Europe as the standard of the religious life.

Indeed, the Holy Rule – it was Benedict himself, modest though he obviously was, who dared twice attach to
it in the text the title of 'holy' – was the first real monastic
rule, previous ones being not much more than in the
nature of admonitions from which the individual abbot
might obtain some guidance or pick up some useful hints.
As such the Rule had no serious rivals, though it should be
added that of set design Benedict did not intend it to be
so hard and fast as to need no further amplification. This
is so far from being the case that throughout Benedictine
history the Rule has always been supplemented with
further regulations, just as some of the provisions it contains have been found inapplicable to modern conditions.

Those Benedictines who, like the Cistercians of the
Reformed Observance (as they now prefer to be known
instead of as Trappists), adhere to a diet that prohibits
all meat except for the sick, may be admirable, but so
strict an enforcement of the Benedictine Rule has not been
considered necessary or even advisable by the main Benedictine body. In the same way the Trappist adhesion to
a well-nigh absolute silence – they are more rigorous in
this respect than even the Carthusians – is to make the
Rule more stringent than Benedict ever intended it to be.
However, just as St Benedict envisaged the possibility that
the austerity he imposed might be softened, so also it could
be argued that he left the abbot free to increase the auster-

ity at his discretion. But the Trappists would say that they are merely returning to the Holy Rule as it left his hands.

The Trappists, however, who contend that theirs is a reversion to the primitive standard, will be discussed later. For the moment the important point to bear in mind is that when the Rule was generally adopted, it was in many communities at first combined with another rule or several others, even in those communities considered as Benedictine. St Benet Biscop drew upon no less than seven rules – or rather the customs of seven different monasteries – yet he is reckoned among the Benedictine saints. The rule of the Irish monk St Columbanus was often used by communities in this way. Nevertheless, it was the Rule of Monte Cassino that supplanted all others in the end. As Dom David Knowles puts it: 'For almost six hundred years, over the whole of civilized Europe outside the Balkans, to be a religious, that is, to serve God according to the Gospel counsels, was to be a Benedictine monk.'

All this tells somewhat against the theory that the Holy Rule was, so to speak, commissioned by the Church. For even if Pope Hormisdas suggested that Benedict compose a rule which might serve other monks as a model, he would never have thought of officially imposing it. Nor was it, in actual fact, taken up except slowly, and in many places, as has been said, only in conjunction with other rules. All this happened after Benedict's death. If the Holy Rule eventually obtained the position that it did, one can only suppose it was because its merits were too evident to ignore.

When St Francis of Assisi managed to obtain tentative approval of the rule he and his disciples proposed to adopt, he was just in the nick of time. Only a short while afterward the Church decreed that new religious institutes

follow one of the already existing rules. This is why St
Dominic, arriving only a few months later with a similar
request, was obliged to adopt the so-called rule of St
Augustine. As a body of legislation this was of such slight
use to the Dominicans that they had to operate upon the
basis of supplementary constitutions, which form the real
rule of their Order. Subsequently the Church's restrictions were relaxed; otherwise there could have been no
distinctive rule for the Jesuits, not to mention other
religious institutes. The point to bear in mind is that St
Benedict produced for the first time what was a piece of
rounded-out legislation rather than a set of recommendations or bylaws or prohibitions. And it was the Holy Rule
that eventually came to be the basis of all monastic
legislation, even such as seemed to resemble it but slightly.

It has been surmised that the Holy Rule owed its success mainly to the lucky chance of St Gregory the Great, a
Benedictine, being elected Pope; such a powerfully
placed personage would naturally use all his influence to
promote the promulgation of the Rule under which he
had lived. But he used this influence so little that it has
even been questioned (by those who misunderstood the
scope of the power of a pope of his day) whether Gregory
was a Benedictine at all. A similar question has been
raised about the monks Gregory sent as missionaries to
England, because in some of their monasteries several
monastic rules were combined. Finally, it has been supposed that if Gregory had been a Benedictine he would
have stressed the Rule more than he did in his *Dialogues* –
which is to forget that he thought of himself as a collector
of the Saint's miracles. Nevertheless, it must be said that
the *Dialogues*, which were immensely popular, did much
to make Benedict known, and hence the Holy Rule. Also,

the missionaries St Gregory sent to England, from which they eventually branched out into other countries, greatly helped to establish the Rule. But none of this would have been of much avail had the Rule not come to be recognized as superior to anything else of its kind. St Gregory's work in this field was probably all the more effective because of being so unobtrusive.

Though the evident superiority of the Rule itself was the main factor in its success, in addition to this one must mention the weight thrown in its favour by Charlemagne and Louis the Pious. As the great Emperor was directing the full force of his administration to ensure order and uniformity in secular affairs, he naturally recognized the value of such conditions in the monastic state, which he saw as a leavening force in society. He had visited Monte Cassino and no doubt saw there the actual manuscript written by Benedict. Certain it is that he was supplied with a careful copy – not, of course, the one made at Aachen in 820, the best copy of the Rule we possess. He was even sent replicas of the measures of bread and wine doled out at Monte Cassino. Through the instrumentality of St Benedict of Aniane (after the chapter of Aachen decided in favour of customs of the mother house) the Benedictine manner of life was assured in the Western Empire. From that date on the Holy Rule completely supplanted all other monastic rules. But all this occurred more than two hundred years after the death of Gregory the Great, although in the intervening time it is probable that the majority of monasteries had already accepted the Rule – in whole or in part – because of its obvious merits.

To say this is not to belittle the lessons either of the Fathers of the Desert or of St Basil or of the great abbots of Gaul. St Martin of Tours, who died in 397, had been taken as the patron of the oratory that Benedict erected at Monte Cassino. John Cassian of Marseilles, who died about 435, was drawn on freely in the Benedictine Rule. One must also mention St Honoratus of Lérins, that famous nursery of Gallic bishops, who died a little before Cassian, and St Caesarius of Arles who died a little before Benedict himself. And of course there were others. The Holy Rule could hardly have found the acceptance it did had they not prepared the ground.

Nor must one omit mention of Cassiodorus, a contemporary of Benedict and perhaps a friend, who, having served as minister of state to the Emperor Theodoric, retired when he was getting on in years to his estates, living there into extreme old age in the community he founded to combine the life of scholarship with that of contemplation, even contemplation (for some) according to the eremitical mode. Nobody will now suggest, I imagine, as was sometimes done in the past that he was a Benedictine, though he may have been glad to adopt (as others did) such parts of the Holy Rule as accorded with a somewhat different purpose. Abbot Chapman is a little hard on this remarkable man, even dubbing him more of a pedant than a scholar. That scholarship was not the sole object of Cassiodorus is evident from the fact that he provided caves for those who wished to live as hermits. His interest in scholarship appears in his having tried to persuade Pope Agapetus to found a Christian university at Rome. And though his literary style may be somewhat precious if contrasted with Benedict's Latin, the word 'pedant' is not justly to be fastened upon a man capable of composing the moving prayer: 'Grant us, O Lord, we beseech Thee, this most glorious and holy vision; let not those, whom Thou hast inspired with so great a longing, be cheated of that boon. May we see Thee alive for ever, who didst deign to die for us; may we see the glory of Thy majesty, who didst will to appear in the lowliness of our flesh. Already here in this present world Thou dost look with loving-kindness on Thy servants; but that they should look upon Thee, that this world cannot give. Grant that grace to Thy faithful, O Lord, in which all rewards are included.'[1] Even though Cassiodorus was not a Benedictine, but rather an adapter of Cassian (an author used by St Benedict himself as a quarry), as Abbot McCann has, I think, conclusively shown as against the speculations of Abbot Chapman, it gladdens one's heart that a man of his wealth and social position should have been willing to renounce it all to follow Christ. There were other men who, even in an age of turbulence, were able to direct their steps into the paths of peace, and only now and then by accident are such devout souls even mentioned by St Gregory, who was not at all concerned with depicting the conditions of the sixth century, or even with recording anything about St Benedict except his miracles. But from the glimpses now and then to be caught of people of this sort, as also from what we know of the eagerness of many men, young and old, to attach themselves to the Saint, we can see that the times, though in many ways evil and disturbed, were ripe for the work he was called by God to perform.

St Benedict himself seems to have been quite uncon-scious of his own importance, for he offers even his Rule rather apologetically, and never thought of it as definitive. The concluding chapter opens: 'We have written this Rule in order that, observing it in monasteries, we may show in some measure that we have good manners and a beginning of religious life.' Could anything be more

[1] Justin McCann's *St Benedict*, p. 204.

disarming? Abbot Delatte is obliged to say: 'Our Holy Father speaks too modestly of his Rule. Is there, apart from the Gospels, a book that has been able, as it has, to adapt itself to all the needs of Christian society from the sixth century to our own day, and which, as God has revealed to certain of His saints, will continue to do so until the coming of the Son of Man?

Six

The *Opus Dei*

WHEN St Paul recommended the singing of 'psalms and hymns and spiritual canticles' he was unquestionably thinking primarily of the Psalter. Few if any hymns have come down to us from the apostolic age, whereas we know that the Christian Church, which sprang up in Judaism and at first used the synagogues for its services, was very familiar with the liturgy of Israel. Moreover, though as has been said, we may find a kind of embryonic monasticism very early, it was for a long time quite un-organized, and in fact can hardly be said to have begun until the fourth century. Even when it did begin there was no Divine Office, or at least no breviary as we know it, but the whole Psalter was said every day.

Today the Church does all it can to foster a liturgical piety, and though most pious Catholics attempt no more (if as much) than to assist daily at Mass, there are more lay people than one would imagine who say some part of the Divine Office and a few who say it all, though they are under no obligation to do so. And a great many recite particular psalms which make some special appeal to them. The riches to be found there are such as to make a powerful appeal even to those who are not Christians at all. The psalms constitute, to begin with, a Jewish book, and King David is one of the greatest heroes not only to the Jews but to the Moslems. Furthermore, he strikes a responsive note in many unexpected quarters – or many we might think unexpected – as do all the famous books of spiritual wisdom. Thus I remember that when my father, who was a missionary in India, made a Brahmin convert – and one of that caste very rarely leaves his ancestral religion – the only consolation the youth's heart-stricken father could find was in reading the psalms of David. They make up in truth one of the world's universal books. The Church in adopting the psalms as its own has drawn out depths never revealed before.

St Benedict's novelty was not in using the psalms, for that had been done by all monks, but in arranging them better, even while largely following the usage of Rome and Milan. Yet though he ordained that the entire Psalter be said every week, instead of daily as by the Desert Fathers, he does not specially insist upon his own arrangement, thereby allowing room for a development which has, in fact, occurred. We can discover from the Holy Rule that there were a day and a night office, but these were not quite as we know them today. Vespers were already said by many communities (Cassiodorus gave them the name of 'Lamp-lighting'), but Compline, with which the office of the day concludes, seems to have been introduced into the Church by Benedict's monks. There are still a number of varieties in the Divine Office. Though the Benedictines say the Roman Mass, their office is somewhat different.

This matter of the Mass is rather surprising, for one might have expected the most ancient of Orders to have devised a mode peculiar to itself, as has been done by some other religious institutes. On one hand we find some of the later Orders retaining the choir to *say* most of the Office rather than *sing* it; on the other hand, the Cluniacs,

like the Trappists and the Carthusians, tend to elaborate.
The Benedictines strike the happy mean between simplicity and solemnity. In any event Benedict made it perfectly clear that the Divine Office, the *Opus Dei*, was
something to which nothing was to be preferred. Though
it would be too much to say that this is their sole reason
for existing – for every religious Order has as its aim the
perfection of its members – the means for Benedictine
perfection lie here.

The first thing to point out about the Benedictine spirit
as we find it in the Holy Rule is that it is quite free of the
subjectivity to be found in much modern spirituality. The
reason for the latter is no doubt due to a considerable
extent to the need for substituting 'devotions' of one kind
or another for the Divine Office, after its solemn public
rendering had been abandoned. This is not to suggest that
such devotions are not all of them good in their way, but
they often incline one to the perfervid and the fussy, so
that now the trend, especially under the guidance of all
the Popes since Pius X, has been toward the liturgy. We
are only now beginning to recover from some of the
effects of the Protestant Reformation, during which, because the liturgy was often impossible to carry out,
Catholics were obliged to substitute something else,
commonly of less value, whatever necessary purpose it
served. In many countries – England and Ireland, for
instance – where it was difficult even to have Mass except
behind locked doors, with sentries posted to give warning
of the approach of pursuivants, worshippers could not do
much more than follow Mass by saying the rosary, an
excellent devotion but one for private rather than liturgical use. And in Ireland Mass often had to be said on an
altar stone in some hidden glen. Moreover, because of the

Reformation, Catholics in their sensitiveness grew intro-
spective. With the suppression of monasteries during
Napoleonic times, the liturgy was largely lost sight of,
except that its main feature, the Mass itself, was of course
retained. The Divine Office was said by priests, only
silently, and often in stealth; its choral recital, so long a
familiar feature of Catholic life, was all but forgotten.

I do not want to be thought of as belittling devotions;
at the same time it must be said that there is the possibility of the soul getting cluttered up with novenas, or of
one's attempting too much along these lines. It might be
better if some people said fewer prayers and lived in the
spirit of prayer. Abbot Butler ventures to deplore some
marks of modern spirituality: 'Its methods of meditation,
its marking progress in virtue, its conscious advancement
in perfection, even its daily charts of defects and acts of
virtue and mortification, and its preference of private
over common prayer.' Though few carry matters to such
an extreme, and it would seem the Abbot is exaggerating
in seeing in this 'a reversion to the earlier monachism of
Egypt', his criticism holds some truth. Even an earlier
Benedictine, the seventeenth-century Augustine Baker,
in his classic *Sancta Sophia*, sometimes succumbs to the
spirit of his day when he writes: 'Since it cannot be denied
that to persons far more distracted by studies than
anciently they were by [physical] labours, which did not
hinder a moderate quiet attention to God, vocal prayer
has not ordinarily sufficient force to recollect the mind
habitually.' While writing in this vein (he says much the
same in other passages) Father Baker, though among the
most outstanding of Benedictine spiritual writers and one
who must be said to be permeated with the Benedictine
spirit, is not really Benedictine at all.

Father Baker does not, of course, deny that this could not be said of St Benedict's day, but he is merely speaking as a man of his unhappy post-Reformation times. The value of private prayer was indeed stressed by the Holy Rule, though without any recommendations as to how best it be made except the suggestion that ordinarily it should be brief. Abbot Butler puts the whole question admirably when he writes: 'The more we are penetrated by the spirit of the liturgy, the better shall we be able to reach the heights of interior prayer; the more sedulously we cultivate mental prayer the more spiritual and contemplative will our recitation of the office become.' It was Our Lord Himself who gave a special promise to the 'two or three' gathered together in His name, not to the man who retires to his room for private prayer, though he, too, is encouraged. Even when prayer is vocal, or even unspoken, there have been those who at the first words of the Our Father have found it impossible to proceed any further, so flooded are their minds with sweetness, and I have heard of an Eastern mystic who for many years had only one prayer, 'O God, be merciful to me a sinner,' thereby reaching sanctity.

Possibly the best thing written on the subject are the two chapters on the *Opus Dei* in Abbot Marmion's *Christ, the Ideal of the Monk*. He starts by pointing out that while every kind of work may be very pleasing to God – as George Herbert sings:

> *Who sweeps a room, as for Thy laws,*
> *Makes that and the action fine –*

yet such works procure God's glory only indirectly, not of themselves but through the intention of those who perform them, whereas the praise of God seeks His glory

directly. Very profoundly and beautifully Marmion passes
from such considerations to remind us that Christ, the
Word, is the canticle that ever ravishes the heart of the
Father, and that as Christ has assumed humanity and has
made all Christians part of His Mystical Body, we can
partake in the offering of this praise. 'The office,' he continues, 'is the official voice of the Bride of Christ. . . .
She sings, united to Christ, under God's very gaze. . . .
Such is the fundamental reason of the transcendency of
the *Opus Dei*; such is the incommunicable and untransfer-
able privilege attached to this prayer, the Work of God,
accomplished with Christ in His name, by the Church,
His Bride.'

All Christians can and should (and in fact must) share
in this to some extent, but there are those specially dedi-
cated to this work – Abbot Marmion is careful to say
that they need not necessarily be Benedictines. Instead, he
quotes Pius X: 'The active participation of the faithful in
the sacred mysteries and in the public and solemn prayer
of the Church is the first and indispensable source whence
is drawn the true Christian spirit.' But though that great
Pope was well aware that what is most ordinarily to be
expected of Christians is their assistance at Mass (not
merely their presence at it, or a mere hearing of it), he
had in mind something more, something that usually can
only be looked for from religious.

As for monks themselves the Abbot writes that it is
impossible for them to be devoutly assiduous at the 'Work
of God' without gaining in a short time a great knowledge of the divine perfections. If we try to 'arrange' our
own lives there is grave danger of shipwreck. 'We must
go in the way of the Church, ever bearing in mind the
words of the Mass, *Per Ipsum, et cum Ipso, et in Ipso*.' If

Christ Himself often recited the words of the psalms, so also, he says, should we strive to give our lives a liturgical pattern.

It may, however, be objected that the recitation of the Divine Office may become formal. And it must be admitted that formality is always a real danger to true spirituality. To some extent it must be admitted that formality threatens every human activity. A man kisses his wife good-bye in the morning while his thoughts are on selling a certain number of paper boxes that day; it may happen that a priest says Mass as a matter of routine. Human frailties must be allowed for; earth, after all, is not heaven. As Lionel Johnson makes heartrending plaint:

> *Could we but live at will upon this perfect height,*
> *Could we but always keep the passion of this peace.*

Alas, we cannot. We cannot for an instant suppose that even St Benedict or the great St Teresa, or Thomas à Kempis did not have their flat and dull periods. Shakespeare was not always spouting sonnets; Homer proverbially nods. Of course monks are mostly very ordinary people; only now and then can any of them have their great moments. It is enough for them, however, that they obey their Rule. More than any other class of men will this lead them to the attainment of the 'perfect height'.

It is also a matter of experience that in private prayer the mind is liable to wander, and this must occur in the chanting of the Divine Office, though it is less likely there because of its being done in common. As for distractions, Father Vincent McNabb, the famous English Dominican, used to say in chapter: 'If you don't have distractions, it's your own fault,' meaning that a man who was busy would have his mind occupied even in choir with other concerns.

But even supposing that distractions could be excluded, the choral Office might still be said in a bovine fashion, and on this the Rule has something to say. St Benedict remarks that 'God is everywhere, but especially when we are assisting at the Divine Office.' And St Thomas Aquinas says something further on the kind of attention necessary. There is first attention to the words sung (or said); it is for this beginners must first strive. There is secondly attention to the *meaning* of the words. But finally (and most important of all) there is attention to God Himself. All three methods are good, and the first usually includes the other two, though I am told that nuns who recite the Divine Office in Latin without much understanding of that language sometimes achieve the third with only a vague knowledge of what it is they have recited. If so, they achieve the main result by by-passing all else. But this is not the Benedictine ideal, as that supposes attention both to the words and their meaning. What is being recited kindles the mind, or so soaks it with inflammable material that at last fire springs from some thought found there. Even when this does not happen – for there are some minds that do not easily if ever catch fire – there is at least a gradual enrichment, even though this may come unperceived.

It is rather hard for us to visualize that in Benedict's time there were few priests among his monks. Though his Rule does mention them, insisting that they be treated just like other monks and have no special privileges, even that none of them should venture to say Mass without the abbot's explicit permission, it seems likely that at Subiaco Mass was said only on Sunday (and perhaps Saturday) and then perhaps by some 'secular' priest who served as chaplain. Later, however, priests did present themselves to the

community for admission, and if additional priests were
needed it was always possible for the abbot to ask a
bishop to ordain them. Benedict is careful to say that no
monk should ask for the priesthood but leave it all to the
abbot's judgment. There can be no question but that the
Holy Rule presupposes a lay community, presided over
by a lay abbot. Today it is taken for granted that every
choir monk should become a priest; at that time the
monastic and the clerical states were quite distinct, even
though the distinction was soon lost.

As lay brothers were a later innovation, all the monks
were expected to do some sort of work, and usually of a
manual sort. From the outset, however, apart from the
monks who had special duties to perform, a certain number had to be assigned to the copying of books – needed
both in the choir and the library – and others who had
useful handicrafts were encouraged to practice these
(under due restrictions). Furthermore, it is clear from the
Rule that all served a week in turn in the kitchen or as
servers at meals. But before long this process was
changed, for we know from Paul Wanefrid's late eighth-
century commentary that there was a daily conventual
high Mass, though this does not prove that even at that
date the majority of monks were priests or on their way
to the priesthood. The Venerable Bede, a monk from the
age of seven, was not 'priested', as he himself tells us,
until he was thirty-five. Yet he had been declared a
Doctor of the Church.

St Benedict's legislation in the matter appears in Chapter XL of his Rule: 'If anyone of the priestly order ask to
be received into the monastery, let not assent be too
quickly granted him; but if he strongly persist in this request, let him know that he must keep all the discipline of

the Rule, and that nothing will be relaxed in his favour.'
Furthermore, if there is a question of any appointment,
the priest-monk must not expect that he will obtain it by
virtue of his ordination, but in every respect, except for
the duties of the altar, he will be promoted by the abbot
only according to the merits of his life. Again in Chapter
LXII Benedict warns: 'Let him who is ordained beware of
arrogance and presume to do nothing that is not commanded by the Abbot, knowing that he is now all the more
subject to regular discipline. Let him not take occasion of
his priesthood to forget the obedience and discipline of
the Rule, but advance ever more and more in the Lord.'

The point is unmistakably clear: Benedict was glad to
have a few priests in the community (one gathers that
they were only a handful), but this was mainly because
priests were needed. Even so they had to be more amenable
to control than would have been secular chaplains not
living in the monastery. Benedict's experience of priests
(if based upon his relations with Florentius) was not very
fortunate. But he also believed that a good priest would
be likely to consider himself entitled to special privileges.
For this reason only carefully chosen men – above all
men of great humility – were admitted.

There is nothing in the Holy Rule that deals specifically
with what chant was to be used by Benedict's monks; this
presumably was considered unnecessary since they no
doubt used what was in vogue. It was St Gregory the
Great who codified 'Ambrosian' plain song, utilizing also
the Roman mode. He gave it the name it now commonly
bears, but versatile as he was, the work was done by
specialists under his direction. The Gregorian reform
naturally based itself also on Benedictine usage, eliminat-
ing many of its crudities and substituting a delicate

balance. The Middle Ages contributed little to its further development, and the modern return to the Gregorian mode – this on the part of all religious Orders where the Office is chanted in choir – shows what beauty was achieved. Trained singers (if they are of a very special kind, such as those of the Pius X School of Music of Manhattanville) may render this chant with great effectiveness, but it is very doubtful whether even they can do so well as the full-throated choir of an abbey habituated to sing the Office every day in the year. Nevertheless, such choirs are able to reach effects that are most stirring. Plain chant, though not indeed 'foolproof', is undoubtedly the most serviceable of all musical systems, as used by a community in which two choirs answer one another. The reason lies not merely in the music itself but in the wholeheartedness from which it springs, the spiritual fervour behind it.

The translation of the psalms into the Vulgate wisely retained one of the distinctive features of Hebrew poetry, and this parallelism could be used in the responses of the choir with striking resonance. In the creation of the chant the Benedictine monasteries played a very prominent role. Yet in this they were perhaps not aiming so much at artistic effect as at meeting a situation they found to exist; thus they discovered that the praises of God uplifted the heart more when they were sung than when they were merely spoken, especially when they were sung by a group of strong, grave voices. What happened was so natural as to be almost inevitable.

In the Desert it would seem that one monk chanted the psalms, while the others listened, meanwhile weaving their baskets, since this called for no conscious attention. But the whole group prostrated themselves in silence at intervals, the intervals being every three psalms. Perhaps this is why St Benedict wrote in Chapter LII: 'Let the oratory be what it is called; and let nothing else be kept there.' No doubt he was thinking of rushes, but some have suggested with a touch of humour that he meant the oratory was not to be a dormitory. But indeed the liturgy he prescribed would have served to keep the brethren awake, as the alternation of choirs assured attention. However, this was no innovation of his but common practice throughout the West.

Even here Benedict laid down no iron-clad regulations. Instead, he wrote in Chapter XVIII: 'Above all, we recommend that if the arrangement of the psalms [which he took pains to give carefully] be displeasing to anyone, he should, if he think fit, order it otherwise; taking care especially that the whole Psalter of a hundred and fifty psalms be recited every week, and always be begun afresh at the Night Office on Sunday. For those monks who show themselves too slothful in the Divine Office, who say in the course of the week less than the entire Psalter, with the usual canticles, show too lax a service; since we read that our holy fathers resolutely performed in a single day what I pray we tepid monks may achieve in a whole week.' Yet while holding up the practice of Egypt for admiration, St Benedict does not seriously wish that Egypt be taken as a model at Monte Cassino. His object is moderation.

As to how the Divine Office should be said Benedict writes in the next chapter: 'We believe that the divine presence is everywhere, and that the Lord beholds the good and evil in every place. Especially do we believe this, without any doubt when we are assisting at the Work of God.' The incidental ceremonies therefore, even the smallest of them, were to be carried out carefully and exactly, yet without parade-ground stiffness. The choir

was to be a school of good manners, not of the external
and empty sort that may mean nothing, but of the good
manners that flow from charity. The same is true on the
altar at Mass, especially high Mass.

Finally we may note this passage in Chapter XLIII:
'Should anyone come to the Night Office after the *Gloria*
of the ninety-fourth psalm (which for this reason we wish
to be said very slowly and protractedly), let him not
stand in his order in the choir, but last of all, or in the
place set apart by the Abbot for the negligent ones, so
that he may be seen by him and by all, until, the Work of
God being ended, he may do public satisfaction.' At
lauds the fiftieth psalm was similarly to be drawn out so
as to give every chance to laggards. St Benedict makes
allowances for human weaknesses, though when they go
beyond a certain point he administers a penance, not as a
rule a very severe one, for he was not a martinet.

He explains not his indulgence (for that is self-evident),
but his reason for imposing the penance, 'that being seen
by all, they may amend for very shame. If they were to
remain outside the oratory, there might be one who
would return to his bed and sleep, or else sit and give
himself to gossip, thus providing an occasion to the evil
one. Let him therefore enter, that he may not lose the
whole, and may amend for the future.' In supposing there
could be only one such loiterer Benedict is being gently
humorous, for one monk could hardly gossip to himself,
though of course he might slip off to bed. However late a
monk might be for the Office, he was expected to put in
an appearance, on the principle that even as a late-comer
he would derive some profit from the *Opus Dei*.

Seven

Benedictine Vows

BEFORE St Benedict introduced them there do
not seem to have been any monastic vows. We have seen
that when he left Enfide and took up his abode in the cave
in the cliff near Subiaco, by accepting the sheepskin *melota*
from the monk Romanus he considered himself irre-
vocably committed to the religious state, and was so
considered by others. But that even this was not always
looked upon in such a stringent sense comes out in a story
told of Macarius, one of the Desert Fathers. Two young
men asked this celebrated solitary whether they might join
him, but he, seeing they were delicately nurtured, yielded
only after they told him that if he refused them they would
have to go to some other solitary. Yet he let them stay only
because he quite expected them soon to withdraw. It is
evident he would not have blamed them had they done so.

One also gathers that many men who become hermits
eventually abandoned the life as too hard. But though the
melota was supposed to bind upon its acceptance, there
were few if any definite regulations. What Benedict did
was to introduce – though only after some experience –
not only vows but what we should call a novitiate. Neither
was hedged around with the safeguards later introduced
by canon law, but he laid down the foundations of these.

One feature Benedict permitted was the donation to
the abbey of children by their parents or of slaves by their
masters. A father, it must be remembered, under the civil

law as it was then, had powers over his children that would be unthinkable today. Yet before we express our horror too loudly a few facts might be considered.

Though ghastly mistakes have been made in such matters – even by pious parents of today who are overly eager to hurry their children into the clerical state – Abbot Herwegen writes that 'from the text of the Rule it cannot be concluded for certain whether or not the boy was bound absolutely and forever by this oblation. The Rule of St Basil, which gives the general practice of the Church, secures to the oblate a decisive choice between the cloister and the world when he came of age, and we see no imperative reason to interpret otherwise the views of St Benedict, although this has sometimes been done and not without harshness.'

That is kind and sensible though the conclusion of Abbot Delatte's commentary on Chapter LIX may be still better. Delatte writes: 'When Tertullus, the senator, offered his young son Placid to St Benedict, he did not think he was acting tyranically; he believed that he was thus securing the safety and eternal life of his son; and he persuaded himself that neither the child nor God would blame him for his decision. As a matter of fact, the majority of children offered in this way afterward joyously clung to the profession that had been made for them. And if there were some who would have gladly returned to the world, are they much to be pitied for having been constrained to remain with God? And instead of letting our minds be possessed by the abuses and inevitable defections caused by the system should we not rather bless it for having given us St Maurus, St Placid, the Venerable Bede, St Gertrude, and so many others? So we have no reason to be ashamed of the fifty-ninth chapter. Had it been applied to ourselves, we should have known God only, for we should have no memories but of Him, we should have nothing to unlearn: where would be the misfortune?' Nevertheless, the Council of Trent refused to acknowledge the validity of any profession made before the completion of one's sixteenth year, or of perpetual vows until one is at least twenty-one.

So much for boy-monks: a much more important consideration is the nature of Benedictine vows. Ordinarily a religious explicity binds himself to poverty, chastity, and obedience, and though these are now taken by Benedictines, at the outset they were considered to be an integral part of the vow of conversion of manners. There has been much argument as to whether this should rather be *conversatio morum* (or shall we say 'monasticity'?) rather than *conversio morum*. But now the question seems to have been decided by Abbot McCann when in a note on page 196 of his recent edition of the Holy Rule he reverses himself in favour of 'conversion of manners', the other presenting too many difficulties. The point is that the early Benedictines merely vowed to become monks, taking everything else to be implied by that.

The main thing in the Saint's mind was that, in addition to the monk's binding himself to conversion of manners (or the mode of monastic life) he also bind himself to 'stability'. Benedict had seen or read a great deal about wandering monks, religious vagabonds, who were monks only in name. Therefore he introduced a feature that a monk make his vows for a particular abbey, the one in which he undertook to live for the rest of his life. The result is that Benedictines have for many centuries obligated themselves not merely to the two things already mentioned but take five vows, these two and the classic three.

Indeed, Benedict's treatment of the standard principles of religious life is so comprehensive as to be the great handbook on the subject – especially as regards obedience and poverty, for chastity he leaves on one side as not calling for specific exposition, so inconceivable does he consider any breach of it to be. Here his silence is perhaps more eloquent than any words than one might use.

In his view everything depends upon a monk's living not only under the direction of the abbot but under the direction of such minor superiors as the abbot may appoint. He goes even a little further, for Chapter LXXI of the Rule enjoins the monks 'to obey one another'. His monks should be eager to oblige, kind and courteous, for akin to formal obedience is fraternal charity. So in Chapter LXIII we find: 'Let the younger brethren, then, reverence their elders, and the elders love the younger.' In short, it is impossible to follow the Rule without becoming a gentleman of the very finest type.

Benedict, however, being a legislator, is not willing to let the matter rest there but is in many places very definite in his rulings. Obedience comes into almost every chapter of the Rule; the one on humility starts off with, 'The first degree of humility is obedience without delay.' What he wanted was a prompt, willing, and whole-hearted response, and this because monastic obedience is primarily obedience toward God. This does not mean, of course, that no representation about the difficulty or impossibility of carrying out an order was ever to be made. But even in such a case a man should at least try to do what he could. Knowing men as he did, Benedict was humorously aware that a high percentage of them are likely to seek the evasion of a difficult task by declaring that it was something that could not be done.

St Benedict rightly considered that the kind of obedience acceptable to God and sweet to man is when what is commanded be done 'not fearfully, tardily, nor lukewarmly, nor with murmuring'. In several places he says that the very worst spirit that can come into a community is one of disaffection and grudge. A monk may carry out the letter of an order in such a way as to make it of slight value to himself, and even of much harm to the brethren among whom he lives, if he makes it apparent that he thinks the order foolish or needless. Of those monks who make excuses for the duties they dodge Benedict speaks with a severity he rarely shows, though even these he sought to bring to a better frame of mind before proceeding to punishment. In the last resort a refractory monk was to be expelled before he infected the rest.

With regard to Benedictine poverty it must be said that it is today regulated by canon law, by the statutes of each congregation, and by the customs of each house. The Holy Rule accordingly is not the only norm, though it is the only standard that it is feasible to consider here. About it Benedict had a good deal to say, as he realized that the heart of man is prone to seek possessions. For instance, in Chapter XXXIII he writes: 'Above all let the vice of private ownership be cut off from the monastery by the roots. Let none presume to give or receive anything without leave of the Abbot, or to keep anything of their own, either book or writing-tablet or pen, or anything whatever; since they are permitted to have neither body nor will in their own power.' That sounds drastic yet is much less so than the concept of poverty held by some other religious orders. St Francis of Assisi, for extreme example, attempted to make poverty well-nigh absolute and took a line that simply had to be modified, though this was largely done by a species of legal fiction, as when the title to friaries was registered in the name of a third party. Yet to this day poverty remains the distinctive Franciscan ideal, and in fact inspires countless thousands of other souls.

The difference between the Benedictines and Franciscans is broadly this: each believes in poverty, yet Benedictines as a corporate group may possess a good deal, even though the individual monk owns nothing, whereas among Franciscans the community itself seeks destitution. Yet the strict theory in either case cannot be fully carried out; I may illustrate this by saying that because of the complexity of modern life the Franciscan friar has to have a certain amount of pocket money and may even have a car assigned to his use. On the other hand, the grandeur of some medieval abbeys would now be regarded as more or less scandalous, and the ownership of slaves by monks would simply not be tolerated, even if any wished to have them. Though slaves are not mentioned as such by Benedict, Abbot Chapman has shown that some of the foundations of the sixth century received donations of slaves as part of their endowment. Servitude was part of the social institutions of the time; it was not part of Benedict's mission to tilt against a condition everywhere taken for granted.

But Benedict was so zealous about the personal poverty of his monks that in Chapter LV he enjoined the abbot frequently to search the beds of the monks, as that was the only place they could hide anything. Yet all were supplied with a sufficiency and the Rule was most careful of those in poor health, or of tender years or who had reached old age. There was to be no rigid uniformity but the abbot was to be for all a kind father, using a wise discretion, never forgetting that, either for being too stern or too lax, he would have to render an account at the judgment seat of God.

Benedict himself had worn a sheepskin *melota* in his cave. But now he adopted a garment more resembling a habit, woven of a rough material, with sleeves reaching to the hands, and a hood. A scapular 'for work' is mentioned, and though just what this was is not certain, we know that it was in some way useful for toil in the fields. (It was not the modern scapular.) In general the dress does not seem to have been very different from the ordinary peasant garb, except that in some way it did show the wearer to be a monk.

For a long time now there have been Benedictines who wear a white instead of the usual black habit. The Rule does not treat the question as very important. Indeed, grey and brown must have been indifferently used at first, the Rule merely prescribing that the dress of the monks should be made of the cloth most cheaply to be bought in the region. Still, it is evident that St Benedict wished his sons to be reasonably well clad, for he enjoins that whenever they go on a journey they wear something a bit better than their ordinary dress, returning this to the vestiarius when they arrived home. On such occasions, too, they were to be supplied with drawers and hose, for like most people of the time who wore long garments, they did not ordinarily have underclothes. Nowhere is there any suggestion that they go barefoot or even in sandals.

Again there is a difference from both earlier and later monastic practice. One of the Fathers of the Desert said that the cloak of the monk should be of such a kind that if it was dropped on the ground, it would be left lying there for three days before any passer-by thought a worth picking up. St Francis of Assisi usually wore it patched habit, and one even derives the suspicion that some of his followers, in imitation of him, stitched quite unneeded patches on their own. It was the same with the young lawyers of the sixteenth century, who, noticing that the Lord Chancellor, Sir Thomas More, was careless about the way he wore his robes – which were rich enough – were also studiously *dégagé*. Benedict expected his monks to be neat and not to keep their habits until quite worn out, but to hand them over to the monk in charge of the wardrobe and receive a new outfit. In all this we see Benedict's sober good sense.

A time came when such regulations were too liberally interpreted. Chaucer's monk even lined his sleeves with fur. It need hardly be said this was utterly at variance with the spirit of the Holy Rule, and so probably was the wealth acquired by some of the medieval monasteries. It was a specious argument to hold that the Benedictine legislation was directed only against personal property and permitted great corporate possessions. Though the monk may have held this or that article only *ad usum*, it was unfortunate that he did so in a wealthy monastery (still professing poverty), for scandal was given, with results which might have been foreseen. Monastic possessions offered a temptation that the rich and powerful could not resist.

Before St Benedict legislated, it was considered that the mere entering of a monastery was an irrevocable commitment. He saw to it that there was a definite probationary period, during which the novice was free to depart. He even kept applicants waiting at the gate to test their sincerity. Today, though the length of the period of probation varies from Order to Order within limits, and is always subject to canon law, the whole concept of

a probationary period stems from St Benedict, and all
Orders model themselves in this respect upon his Rule,
even while introducing their own modifications.

In his modesty St Benedict several times apologizes for
his moderation, though it is now the thing most universally praised in him. His was only 'a little rule' and for
'beginners'. But in it he gauged human nature with won-
derful accuracy, curbing at the same time the excesses of
individualism and the enervation of laxity. Experience
has amply shown that if the 'little' he called for is faithfully performed, spiritual heights may be reached. Benedict's apologies are really unnecessary.

The question may now be asked whether those religious who live under the Holy Rule incur sin by its
infraction. They are bound in this way by their vow but
not by the Rule itself, except, of course, where breaches
of morals are concerned. 'Show me a man who has observed his rule perfectly and I will canonize him,' said
one of the Renaissance popes with some jocularity but
also with much wisdom. It would, in fact, be very difficult
to avoid minor infractions of a religious rule – Benedict's
or any other. Such infractions may be punished, severely
or not, according to the gravity of the offence. Thus a
man who arrives late for meals or the choir receives a
small penance, but persistent negligence in this matter
could take on the character of disobedience and so become sin; in ordinary cases it is merely a fault that cannot
be called even venial sin.

To return to a feature peculiar to Benedictine life, but
essential to it: the vow of stability. This means that the
monk undertakes to live until death in the abbey which
has received him, and in which he has been professed.
Though it is not impossible for a monk to be transferred

from one abbey to another, this must be with his abbot's permission and with his own consent. When such a transference occurs, his stability is transferred to the new abbey he joins.

Such a vow is not at all suitable for every form of religious life. The Orders of friars that arose in the thirteenth century did not wish their members to wander at large according to their own sweet fancy, but they had to be mobile, sent anywhere according to the judgment of their local superiors. It is so with the Jesuits and most of the later congregations; they are attached to a province and to no particular house. Though before very long we find Benedictines doing a great deal of missionary work, they established abbeys wherever they could. When they could not do so, but perforce became temporary free lances, they returned to their cloister as soon as possible. The principle of stability was not lost by them.

At Monte Cassino a monk spent all his days within the bounds of the abbey property. He went out to work in the monastic fields, but returned to the choir for the choral Office and to the cloister for study and meals and sleep. Now and then business of one sort or another might take a couple of monks away for a few days, but all excursions merely for pleasure were discountenanced. Nor had the monk any social life, except what he found among his brethren. He followed a round of prescribed duties, but though the Rule provides for no period of relaxation (and kept him so busy that it is not easy to see when this could have been obtained), it may be confidently assumed that a regular opportunity for recreation was granted. A man as wise and fatherly as Benedict would have seen the need for it.

Two things should again be stressed. The first is that

the Saint, while praising the life of hermits, and even seeming to regard it as something to which his cenobites might graduate, did not provide for anything but a community in his Rule. We hear of his going to a local hermit named Martin who had chained himself to the rock of the cave in which he lived. Benedict, though he had no authority over this man, except that of his spiritual prestige, told him to take off his chains. He did not, however, tell him to leave his cave. The point he made was that not chains but the love of God should hold the hermit there. The advice was no doubt offered with a smile, but Martin saw the common sense in what the Saint had said; therefore he obeyed.

The other point is that though Benedict inculcated the practice of silence, it is evident from passages scattered here and there throughout the Rule that he did not think of making this absolute. After Compline it was to be as nearly perfect as possible, but when the monks rose in the small hours to begin their Office, the prompt risers were instructed to urge the laggards to get up. This may sometimes have been done merely by shaking them, but one gathers that speech was permitted if necessary. Certainly Benedict's reproof against those who, because they were late, stayed outside the choir gossiping indicates talk – talk which aggravated their offence. But in the chapter on humility we find: 'The eleventh degree of humility is that when a monk speaks he does so gently and without laughter, humbly, gravely, and with few and reasonable words, and that he be not noisy in his speech.' In short, Benedict did not forbid either talk or laughter, but only the boisterousness of the clown. A pleasant wit, as the Abbot Delatte was to say, could grace the cloister. St Benedict, who himself shows that he had a good deal of quiet humour, would have agreed with the dictum of St Teresa of Avila: 'Heaven preserve us from solemn saints!'

Finally in Chapter XLVIII, Benedict ordained that two seniors be appointed to go the rounds during the reading periods (about five hours a day) to see that none of the monks were wasting their time in idle chatter. He adds in the same chapter that 'one brother shall not associate with another at unsuitable hours' – a plain indication that there were hours considered suitable for such association. It even suggests fixed periods for recreation.

One concludes that, apart from the vows, a rather wide liberty was permitted. Therefore Abbot (the later Cardinal) Gasquet in his long introduction to Montalembert's *Monks of the West* writes that St Benedict's object was in many respects quite different from the rigid uniformity that appeared at the beginning of the ninth century. This Gasquet describes: 'There was designed to be uniformity in the quantity of food and drink, uniformity in the time of rising and going to rest, uniformity in their church services and their choir ceremonies, uniformity in the length and cut of the habit: in a word absolute uniformity in everything.' The monastic system owes a good deal to the German St Benedict of Aniane, but under his reforms in the time of Charlemagne it became rigid, though fortunately later regained most of its former flexibility. The Holy Rule remained and is now better observed than ever before. This means an orderly observance but without pedantry, so that we see Benedictines of the twentieth century carrying out the essential ideas of the founder. What had been outmoded is abrogated, and the addition of supplementary Constitutions make the Rule all the more applicable to the conditions of our time so that the original concepts of St Benedict have become all the clearer and stronger.

Eight

The Abbot

A superior is an obvious necessity for a religious community, but as a Benedictine abbot has a special character and responsibility indicated in the Holy Rule these had better be indicated at this point, especially as so much hinges upon them. In the Desert, where there were hardly more than clusters of hermitages, the title of abbot seems to have been conferred upon any holy old monk and did not indicate authority so much as respect. Even when the cenobitic system began to emerge, first under Pachomius and soon afterward under Basil, the position of the abbot was not very well defined. In Gaul things progressed a good deal further but we get some insight into the state of many of the Italian communities when we read of the amazed resentment of the monks of Vicovaro on discovering that when Benedict reluctantly consented to become their head he really intended to govern. Accordingly they tried to get rid of him by murder. Benedict's conception of the abbot's office was in many ways something new.

St Basil, as Abbot Herwegen points out, wished to establish a relationship of master and disciple, whereas 'it was reserved for St Benedict the Roman to erect the whole structure of the monastic community clearly and distinctly on the principle of paternity'. Yet in this matter Benedict, as usual, draws hints from several sources, especially the letters, canons, and decretals of St Leo, though, as is also usual with him, he gives these a new form. He must not be understood as writing of himself but as setting down directives that might be of service to his successors at Monte Cassino and those elsewhere who chose to use his Rule.

His method of choosing the abbot was new. St Basil would have him selected by the superiors of neighbouring communities; St Benedict would have him elected by the community over which he was to rule. But in Chapter LXIV he writes what seems a bit puzzling: 'In the appointment of an Abbot let this principle be observed, that he be made Abbot who is chosen by the whole community unanimously in the fear of God, or even by a part, however small, with sounder counsel.' Now unanimity can virtually never be expected, and of course any one group could consider itself the 'better part', with the certainty of violent dissensions. We must therefore suppose that Benedict meant that the barest majority would suffice.

An Abbot is elected for life, though ordinarily when he becomes too old for efficient work he is glad to have a co-adjutor. Though in some countries a set term has been introduced, it is worth noting that in the United States, where one might expect to find this procedure followed, there is adherence to the idea of perpetuity. Abbot Butler, writing as Abbot of Downside, says: 'When I was a young man an elder father described the then-existing quadrennial system as a year of enthusiasm, a year of disillusionment, a year of work, and a year of looking forward to a change.' For one reason or another St Benedict's ideas as to the mode of appointing an abbot are not everywhere adhered to, but there is no doubt as to what those ideas are. However, here as elsewhere, he was indicating general lines of procedure rather than insisting upon an iron-clad law.

Should by some ill chance the wrong man be elected – perhaps one who, once in power, uses it arrogantly or incompetently – this does not mean that he must be endured until he dies. In such an event the abbots of the district have the right to remove him, or the bishop may, or (this does seem surprising) the pious layfolk of the neighbourhood may intervene to change a scandalous situation. Centuries later both the groups of Cluny and Citeaux managed matters so as to be amenable only to the Pope. In sixteenth-century England there were only five 'exempt' monasteries of 'black' monks, and not a great many in France, whereas in the United States at present all the abbeys are exempt from episcopal control. Benedict was writing only of what seemed to him most feasible in his day.

It might also happen that a depraved (or perhaps we had better say 'relaxed') community would elect a certain abbot, as the Abbot Delatte suggests, because it could say: 'Look at his habits, look how he is involved in the same failings as ourselves; he is a monk who will not be troublesome; we may make him Abbot without fear.' This possibility is not very likely, but is conceivable. It is among the reasons why Benedict indicates in the Rule methods for getting rid of the unworthy head of an abbey.

But such considerations are largely hypothetical. The Benedictine community is above all else a family, animated by the family spirit. This is what gives it its grace and charm. Yet it differs from the family in one important respect: in nearly every family in the ordinary course of events the children leave home, and while they may retain great affection for the family circle, only now and then do they return. In the monastic family, on the other hand, there is no severance except the one that comes with

death. The attachment of all the members to one another
can only grow stronger and deeper with the passage of
time.

Yet though the system is essentially patriarchal, there
have been some Benedictine authors (and one has to include even the wise and learned Abbot Butler among
them) who exaggerate a little in describing the abbot as a
kind of benevolent monarch. Even if the Benedictine
form of government is not 'democratic' in the commonly-
used sense, except that the abbot is elected by his monks,
he works within the framework of a rule and is, as we
have seen, removable. In short, wide as are the abbot's
powers, their bounds are fixed.

The Holy Rule further provides that there should be a
council – to which the whole community should ordinarily be summoned, but which need be attended by only
a few old and sage monks when the question involved is
of special delicacy. At other times Chapter III says that
respectful attention should be paid to the opinions of the
younger monks, 'because it is often to the younger that
the Lord reveals what is best'. After hearing the monks'
advice the abbot is to follow his own counsel.

So far the provisions of the Holy Rule. It should be
added that now canon law and the statutes of each congregation determine what the abbot may or may not do
without the consent of his chapter. This is because a man
who has been a most excellent abbot, and a wise father to
his sons, might develop some weakness that could prove
disastrous. To take an example, he might have an itch to
build on an unnecessarily expensive scale. It would be
quite unfair to have the community burdened long after
his death with the outcome of a whim that might be
merely an expression of personal vanity disguising itself

as zeal in the service of God. So the council or chapter is given a restraining influence. However, taking the abbot's functions in the sense Benedict had in mind, the kind of man described in the Rule would still make most of the decisions after listening to everybody.

The community at Monte Cassino, though not large if compared to some of those of the Middle Ages, must have started with close on to a hundred and fifty monks, if all those at Subiaco followed Benedict there. By the time the Rule came to be written one would guess that the numbers had doubled, though it should be remembered that a second abbey had been founded at Terracina, near Naples, perhaps as a means of cutting down an unwieldy community. As a group of this size could not be effectively governed by one man, Benedict appointed a 'dean' who was to be in general charge of each ten monks. These deans, Chapter XXI says, were to be selected on the basis of holy life rather than of seniority; they were all to be directly responsible to the abbot.

On the other hand, Chapter LXV shows little enthusiasm for the office of prior, Benedict writing there: 'It very often happens that by the appointment of the Prior grave scandals arise in monasteries; since there are some who, puffed up by the evil spirit of pride, and deeming themselves to be second Abbots, take upon themselves an usurped power.' One would gather that this refers to some painful experience of his own. But the difficulty was that at that time the priorship was elective and so more or less independent of the abbot. Later the priors became a settled part of the Benedictine organization, invaluable as second in command, needed to be in control while the abbot was obliged to be away. The deans, on the other hand, the abbot's appointees, whom Benedict preferred as less of a danger to good order, soon disappeared.

Among the most important offices in the abbey was that of the cellarer, the official who in most religious houses and seminaries would now be called the procurator. Chapter XXXI lays down that he must be a member of the community, otherwise there was danger a person from the outside might be brought in to manage affairs because he happened to have great business efficiency. He was to be 'a man wise and of mature character, temperate, not a great eater, not haughty, not headstrong, not offensive, not dilatory, not wasteful, but a God-fearing man, who may be like a father to the whole community'. The list of qualifications is interesting, but Abbot Delatte comments that, though in those barbarous days, a cellarer might take advantage of his opportunities to give himself privileges in the matter of food and drink that could become gluttony, 'nowadays we should be more inclined to advise the Abbot to choose a cellarer who both ate and drank'. Without taking too seriously the complaints made by seminarians that the procurator is trying to ingratiate himself with the bishop by cutting down on supplies – for it is notorious that the young are given to making such complaints – a full-blooded procurator would usually be better than one too stingy.

The official in charge of the farming utensils was admonished to look after them as though they were as sacred as the vessels of the altar. And of course both he and the cellarer in a large abbey were obliged to have assistants or to divide their work. A highly important person was the monk who looked after the wardrobe, for he had to see to it that all the brethren were adequately supplied.

The monks took their turn by each serving as a cook for a week, no doubt several of them at a time. The food was so simple that it did not demand much culinary skill. All this was considered as part of the ordinary manual work, though very early there were servants and even slaves, who were treated as members of the community. Such help was necessary as the monks, or those capable of it, spent a good deal of time copying books rather than in toiling in the fields. The *scriptorium* indeed before long absorbed so much time that in the eleventh century lay brothers were introduced. As a rule they were unlettered, though sometimes they chose this life out of humility. Their habit was slightly different from that of the choir monks and they wore beards, for which reason they were popularly known as the *barbati*, though their official title was that of *conversi*. In some places they even constituted the majority of the religious.

In a large medieval monastery there were also a number of lay folk employed in one capacity or another. Some of these were no doubt merely servants, engaged for menial tasks; a much larger number were the tenants of the abbey farms; finally there was a small proportion of people who acted as overseers or stewards or office workers. Such an organization grew to be a good deal more complex than anything envisaged by St Benedict. Communities of this kind have, of course, long since disappeared, and their precise nature must be largely conjectural. The closest we now come to anything of the sort – and that can hardly be very close – is in the monastic establishments in the United States which have been such a tower of strength to rural communities. But while the holdings in land of such abbeys may be very large, everything is conducted with the utmost simplicity and frugality. The abbot is no longer a territorial magnate, with armed retainers and (as in England) a seat in the House of Lords (though few of these ever existed), but a simple monk hardly to be distinguished from those over whom he rules.

There are a few puzzles in the Holy Rule that have never been quite satisfactorily explained. One of these is what is said in Chapter LVI about the abbot's table, for Benedict says that the abbot should have his meals with his guests. But as elsewhere he tells us that guests are never lacking, how (if his words are to be taken literally) was he ever able to be with the community? Benedict further explains that, as guests were liable to arrive at any time, and almost always unannounced, this is done so as not to disarrange the mealtime *horarium*. There is even to be a special kitchen for the guests – it would presumably serve rather better fare than the monks themselves received. On the other hand, all this may merely mean that while guests were many, they were not a steady stream, but that at some periods of the year they arrived in numbers while at others there were few or none at all. The commentators widely disagree, and where even the learned and judicious Abbot Delatte fails to resolve the mystery, it is hardly for me to grapple with it. But it might be remarked that, whatever past customs may have been, in these days a guest in a Benedictine abbey ordinarily sits beside the abbot in the refectory.

Such a custom is of ancient date, for the Council of Aachen in 817 forbade the abbot to take his meals apart from the community, though we hear that in some places during the Middle Ages the abbot had his own residence, into which he would no doubt invite guests of special importance. Their care, however, eventually devolved upon the guest master, who in many instances would do no more than introduce them to the abbot. But in the nature of things, because of changed conditions in the modern world, the Benedictines are now not under the old need of maintaining what Chesterton has called 'the inns of God, where no man paid', though their tradition of hospitality, as I have had many occasions to discover, is undiminished.

Obviously the abbot could spare relatively little time for his guests. He had his own religious life to live; he had to guide that of all his monks; and he had to be conversant with the material affairs of the monastery. Perhaps even more important than his personal attendance of the choir, and the example he set there, was the spiritual advice he offered those who needed it. He gave, of course, general conferences to all the men under him, but there were also private consultations. This must have been what was in Benedict's mind when he wrote in his famous long chapter on humility: 'The fifth degree of humility is to hide from one's Abbot none of the evil thoughts that beset one's heart, nor the sins committed in secret, but humbly to confess them.' This is what is today termed a manifestation, which all religious are encouraged to make to their superiors, though canon law now forbids any superior to demand that it be given. St Benedict clearly is not referring (at least not in his own case) to sacramental confession, for as he was not a priest he was not qualified for this.

Even in this matter Benedictinism represents a tradition far removed from what Abbot Butler calls 'a fussy, meddlesome direction, so common nowadays'. It was, Butler points out, strongly denounced by St John of the Cross and Father Baker, that eminent Benedictine writer on the spiritual life. Both believed that 'once a soul has been properly started and established in a suitable course of spirituality and prayer, the need of direction becomes rare and confined to great occasions'. It is, of course, only such occasions that Benedict has in mind. When one of his monks is perplexed, to whom would he more naturally turn than to his abbot? He had no intention of forcing confidences, but was merely indicating that when needed the abbot was always available, and that it would be pride not to turn to him.

The question may arise as to what extent the legislator came under his own law. The answer is that just as the superior has power to dispense his subjects from this or that minor provision of the Rule, so also he might dispense himself, though only for such a reason as might apply to others. As Delatte remarks: 'The Abbot is not a legislator [he cannot mean Benedict himself, who certainly was a legislator, but the abbots who adopted his Rule, if only in an eclectic fashion]. Toward the Rule, he has a double obligation: to observe it in his own capacity of monk, to see to its observance in his capacity as Abbot. What authority will his teaching have when his words are on one side and his deeds on the other?' But the limpid sincerity of Benedict is everywhere evident. St Gregory the Great summed it all up when he wrote toward the end of the second book of the *Dialogues*: 'Anyone who wishes to know more about [St Benedict's] life and character can discover in his Rule exactly what he was like as an Abbot, for his life could not have differed from his teaching.' Though Gregory says next to nothing about the Rule itself – his concern being primarily with the Saint's miracles – we amplify at least to this extent: that the Saint's teaching was that the abbot was always to act with discretion, being severe when that was required, mild when that seemed more likely to effect the desired purpose, and that severity was called for only in very rare and exceptional circumstances.

St Benedict himself explained what kind of man the abbot was to be: 'Above all, let him not, overlooking or undervaluing the salvation of the souls entrusted to him, be more solicitous for fleeting, earthly, and perishable things; but let him ever bear in mind that he has under-taken the government of souls of which he shall have to give an account.' But lest zeal should become too offi-cious, he is also told to be moderate in whatever correc-tion he may have to employ, lest in scouring the vessel of its rust he break it.

Such warnings were needed, for St Benedict foresaw that there might be abbots who, though excellent as managers of temporalities, might tend to forget that their spiritual duties were incomparably more important. While true prudence is a moral virtue, much that passes for prudence (both in the eyes of the world and in the eyes of the ecclesiastical world) is often little more than caution, sometimes a caution that forgets God's providence. Bene-dict therefore continued: 'And that he may not complain for want of worldly substance, let him remember what is written: "Seek first the kingdom of God and His justice, and all these things shall be added unto you." ' Even in his time Monte Cassino was a highly complex organiza-tion, and organizations of that sort grew more complex with the passage of time. Yet the abbot was not to be primarily an administrator – though he was obliged to be that, too; primarily he was to be the spiritual father of his monks. They, following the same Rule as he did, were to be led by him from this the home they had chosen on earth to their heavenly home.

Nine

Benedictine Life

THIS CHAPTER will be concerned not with Benedictine life as it was lived during the Middle Ages, nor with Benedictine life today, but with the kind of life lived while St Benedict was at Monte Cassino. And though any description of this must necessarily be drawn from the Holy Rule, we have for it a reliable documentation. If now and then allusions are made to later developments, it will only be by way of illustrating a point. One may say, however, that though Benedictine activity was immensely to broaden, its basis has always been the *Opus Dei*, to which 'nothing is to be preferred'. While a Benedictine monk may have to perform his work for a while in isolation, he cannot be living a full Benedictine life so long as he is deprived of the choral chanting of the Divine Office. Other religious Orders, or some of them, may encourage free-lance work, and may be very useful as such, but of the Benedictine it must be said that his sole object is to serve God in the monastic state, and this, with him, presupposes the choir.

Everybody has heard the maxim *Orare et laborare*. As the kind of prayer Benedict had in mind has been touched upon already (and it may be reverted to again), at this point the kind of work should be stressed. In the beginning it was mainly, and of necessity, manual work, and this of course included such duties as were performed by the cellarer, the keepers of the wardrobe and the farm implements, the monk appointed to serve the door, and the service of the kitchen. However, from the outset a number of monks had to be set aside for the *scriptorium*, which also was looked upon as manual work.

This last was in many ways the hardest work any monk was called upon to do. The accounts left by some of the scribes tell us that, though they used only three fingers, when they ended their labours their whole body was tired. This was even more true when three or four wrote to another's dictation, for choir books had to contain exactly the same number of words on every sheet. This called for an intense and prolonged attention and considerable skill, and accounts for some pages showing the last few lines written very large or very small, so as to spread out or crowd in the words. Uniformity was of the utmost importance.

But the ordinary work of the first monks was that of farming, not mere gardening, real toil. This was necessary not merely for discipline but for the support of the house. However, if a man had special skill in a handicraft he might be permitted to use it, for that also was a source of support, though Benedict laid down the principle that whatever was made was to be sold at less than the current prices. In the simple society of his time this was no doubt praiseworthy, yet today it might be considered as under-selling workers who had to maintain families. Any artificer was to be stopped at once if he began to plume himself upon the income he was bringing in. He might be allowed to resume his trade when he showed himself sufficiently chastened, but not until then.

Such work, not only in St Benedict's time but even

during the age of the great monastic architects, makers
of stained glass or statues, was always anonymous. As
Cardinal Gasquet says: 'In the monastic order the action
of the individual is sunk in that of the corporate body to
which he belongs. It is thus not a single man's peculiar
gifts or talents, but the united reputation of a body of
unknown men which is the power brought by such a
work as that of a people's conversion. Not the men who
compose the monastic corporation, but the life they live,
is the exciting and attractive force. Individual members
pass away, but the self-same life goes on, and the self-
same influence continues to manifest itself on those
brought within its sphere.'

A second thing may be said: though a pattern may be
discerned, throughout the work of the monks, even during the seventh and eighth centuries, we must not expect
to find uniformity. What was true of one place was not
necessarily true of another; that is, one monastery was
often more successful in carrying out the Benedictine ideal
than was another. Here probably nothing better has been
said than what was written by Cardinal Newman. He said:
'Saint Benedict found the world, physical and social, in
ruins, and his mission was to restore it in the way, not of
science but of nature, not as if setting about to do it, not
professing to do it by any set time or by any rare specific
or any series of strokes, but so quietly, patiently, gradually,
that often, till the work was done, it was not known to
be doing. It was a restoration, rather than a visitation,
correction, or conversion. The new world which he
helped to create was a growth rather than a structure.
Silent men were observed about the country, or discovered in the forest, digging, clearing, and building; and
other silent men, not seen, were sitting in the cold

cloister, tiring their eyes, and keeping their attention on the stretch, while they painfully deciphered and copied and recopied the manuscripts which they had saved. There was no one that "contended, or cried out", or drew attention to what was going on; but by degrees the woody swamp became a hermitage, a religious house, a farm, an abbey, a village, a seminary, a school of learning, and a city.'

Nor should it be forgotten that when some of the abbeys became rich, their wealth was almost entirely in their lands and what those lands could produce. Lands of this sort had also usually been some waste tract that nobody had found it worth his while to cultivate, nobody but the monks. Furthermore, a group of men living very simply, wearing inexpensive clothes, eating plain food, drinking little wine, and organized for work, can hardly help becoming corporately wealthy. Yet guests were plentiful, Benedictine hospitality being proverbial, and poorer travellers usually received an alms. Even so, the goods of the abbeys increased, for from the alms that the monks received (mostly stipends for Masses for the departed souls) they acquired more land and with it the opportunity of adding to their wealth.

This wealth, as we shall see, became a danger, not so much because it was a temptation to luxury but because it created in the minds of the rich an incitement to sluice off into their own coffers what the monks had. The argument was that those who were imitating the poverty of Christ had no need of anything beyond bare necessities. A situation came into being very far from anything envisaged by St Benedict, during whose time monks had rarely been able to do more than support themselves with difficulty.

What of the social class from which the majority of

monks came? Abbot Butler in his classic *Benedictine Mon-achism* advances the thesis that, as most of them were peasants, the Holy Rule imposed nothing more austere than what they were already accustomed to, which may be considered as roughly equivalent to the life of the Campanian peasants in the sixth century. Well, if frugality rather than austerity was the aim, the Downside community, which Abbot Butler headed, was justified in its spacious way of life, as its members had virtually all come from well-to-do families. Their mode of life, according to this thesis, was what they were used to, so that anything more severe would exceed Benedictine moderation.

The flaw in the argument, as Abbot Chapman has shown, is that the first monks had few peasants among them, Chapman writing: 'There is no slave, or *colonus* or *rusticus* mentioned. All are nobles – Maurus, Placid, Theoprobus, Speciosus, Gregorius, and the defensor's son – except the middle-class *Curialis* and the lower middle-class (?) Valentinus.' One gathers that St Benedict obtained, for the most part, rather aristocratic followers. While Chapman may be claiming too much, he seems to be nearer the mark than Butler.

In this matter McCann agrees with Chapman, concluding: '[Benedict's] community was in fact a mixed one, but it must have contained a considerable, if not a preponderant, number of monks who derived their origin from the more or less well-educated classes of that day. It was to such people, in fact, that the life of prayer and study enjoined by St Benedict would make its readiest appeal. If the Rule makes special provision also for the illiterate, that very fact would tend to show that such, though certainly there, were yet in a minority.' One might go even further: while a not very well-educated novice

might be admitted to profession at the end of his probationary year, it does not follow that men of this type were
permitted to remain ignorant: at least they could learn
the Office by heart, so as to take their part in the choir,
which took up from three to five hours a day, depending
on the season. Only those able to do this were suited for
the kind of life Benedict had in mind.

The monastery food was simple but sufficient, even
during Lent there being no great austerity. But there was
then only one full meal a day, and at it meat was never
served, except to the sick or old or young. But ordinarily
at least two dishes were provided, so that there might be
a choice. The meal was eaten in silence, except for the
voice of the appointed reader. This reader was appointed
by the abbot, who also selected the books to be read. He,
and the servers – as they would have to wait for the
'second table' – were given a little bread and wine beforehand, by way of fortification. It was not permitted to
attract the attention of the servers making their rounds
by more than a quiet sign, even knocking on the table
being forbidden, so as not to interfere with the silence.

Chapter XXXIX of the Rule lays down that a pound of
bread was to be served daily to each monk and in Chapter
XL Benedict provides that a *hemina* of wine be given, but
it was left to the discretion of the abbot to add to this
amount, if the monk's work had been heavy. Regarding
the wine he tells that, though it is by no means a drink for
monks, 'yet, since in our days they cannot be persuaded
of this, let us at least agree not to drink to satiety, but
sparingly; because wine "maketh even the wise to fall
away".' Perhaps it was with this in mind that Compline,
Benedict's contribution to the Divine Office, opens with
the words of St Peter (I Peter, 5:8): 'Be sober and

watch: because your adversary the devil goeth about as a roaring lion, seeking whom he may devour.'

It is now uncertain as to how large these measures of wine were. Charlemagne obtained replicas of them, which would not have been necessary had they corresponded to the standard in general use. If, as has been argued, the Benedictine pound was sixteen ounces as against the Roman twelve, the Benedictine *hemina* was presumably also larger than the usual *hemina*. But opinions differ as to the quantity, ranging from half to a full pint. Nor is it unlikely that, if some monks took only part of their allotted *hemina* or no wine at all, the servers would have had a second small quantity to distribute. (As they had already received a little wine before the meal began, let us hope they would not have kept for themselves what was left over. We may be quite sure that even a very mild intoxication would have been promptly punished.)

Punishment of various kinds are prescribed by the Rule, but this seems to be rather by way of advice to those abbots who wished to follow in the ways of Monte Cassino than as anything intended as obligatory. Some have unfortunately thought of the Rule as being largely a penal code. There are even pictures that show St Benedict with a ferule in one hand and the Rule in the other. But the rod was reserved for people who, in the judgment of the abbot, could be most effectively amended by this means: adolescents, or the ruder members of the community, or the sullen. Ordinarily, the punishments were light, among the severest being exclusion from the choir or refectory, or both – what was styled 'excommunication'. This does not mean that they were totally excluded but rather that they were present in a place of disgrace. While receiving this punishment, nobody was permitted to hold any communication with the culprit, under pain of himself being excommunicated. In the very last resort, after everything else had been tried, the troublesome monk was expelled. Such a monk would not be re-admitted, but one who left of his own accord might be taken back three times at the discretion of the abbot.

The Holy Rule shows extreme mildness toward the erring, saying in Chapter XXVII: 'The Abbot is bound to use the greatest care [toward them], and to strive with all possible prudence and zeal not to lose any of the sheep committed to him. He must therefore know that he has undertaken the charge of weak souls, and not a tyranny over the strong.' Therefore he should send 'secret consolers' to the excommunicated brother, to sympathize with him and thus to try and bring about repentance, and on the other hand to prevent his being overwhelmed with despair.

Primarily the Benedictine disciplinary regulations are directed against infractions of obedience, though ulti-mately against pride. A rather casual way of doing things may not be too serious if not persistent. For if a monk tries to follow the Rule as perfectly as possible, he will thereby reach humility and through humility Christian perfection. His obedience should be wholehearted, eager, and prompt. Obedience yielded in a grudging way is by no means sufficient and will sooner or later betray itself. It is even likely to end in insubordination. When that happens the monk has to be expelled.

Throughout the Rule humility is stressed and is the special subject of a long chapter. The arrangement of the virtue into twelve successive degrees is not intended to be arbitrary; still less is it needful to reach one degree before passing to the next. But Benedict starts with the fear of the Lord, and this is fundamental and permanent, as even in heaven that fear will remain, mingled with love. The second degree, particularly applicable to those under religious vows, is 'that a man love not his own will'; the third that 'a man for the love of God submit himself to his superior in all obedience'; the fourth that he should embrace what is hard and contrary – even injuries – patiently; the fifth that he should manifest his mind to his abbot; the sixth that he be content with 'the worst and meanest of everything'; the seventh that he should not merely call himself lower and viler than everybody else but really believe this of himself.

Here is a crucial matter, one that embodies plain good sense. St Paul called himself the greatest of sinners though he was one of the greatest of saints. In so doing there was no pose, for a man knows himself better than he knows others. He therefore knows the guilt of his own sins, whereas what is behind even the proved crimes of others is, at least in its circumstances, known only to God. Delatte quotes the Count de Maistre as saying: 'I know not what passes in the heart of a rogue; but there is enough in the heart of a honest man to make him blush.' The prayer we should all pray is, 'O God, be merciful to me a sinner.'

Very far from this is the challenge made by Rousseau in his *Confessions*: 'Gather round me the countless host of my fellow-men; let them hear my confessions, lament for my unworthiness, and blush for my imperfections. Then let each of them in turn reveal, with the same frankness, the secrets of his heart at the foot of the Throne, and say, if he dare, "I am better than that man".' It is a challenge not likely to be accepted, in spite of Rousseau's many weaknesses. His is an inverted humility which says in effect, 'All right, but I'm not worse than are others,' and that is to accuse rather than confess.

The eighth degree of humility is for a monk to do nothing except what is authorized by the Rule. This extends to acts which, however meritorious in themselves, lose their merit for one who has renounced his own will for the common life of the monastery. The ninth degree of humility is to refrain the tongue – not at all times but when talk is inappropriate. Similarly the tenth degree inculcates that a monk be not too easily given to laughter; in short, that Benedict wishes no indulgence in that boisterous buffoonery which so irritates when encountered in the world. In the cloister there should be dignity and restraint, though these do not rule out a harmless jest. The eleventh degree repeats much the same thing: 'that when a monk speaks he do so gently and without laughter, humbly, gravely, with few and reasonable words, and that he be not noisy in his speech.' This might be taken as good manners for everyone; few men are more objectionable than the clown who makes himself the life of the party.

The twelfth and final degree of humility is when a man in his whole demeanour shows that he is suffused with a sense of his littleness in the sight of God. As Delatte puts it: 'If humility be really in the heart it will appear in the body also, and will regulate all its movements; it will be like a new temperament, a nature in humility replacing the old.' He further remarks 'that the eyes of the saints, even when they are looking at some object, seem turned inwards, towards the hidden Beauty, so far and yet so near.' So Benedict says of his twelfth degree that the monk 'should ever think of the guilt of his sins, and imagine himself already present before the terrible judgment seat of God.'

The Benedictine monastery was a co-operative enterprise, which had to support itself by the work of all its
members, even if the same sort of work was not demanded from all. What was also laid down in the Rule was
that set periods be devoted to pious reading, mostly from
the Bible, but with the Fathers of the Church and the lives
of the saints also drawn upon. Some of the older monks
were appointed to see that this regulation was carried
out, so that a man should not sit woolgathering or with
his head on the desk, lost in sleep. Such supervision was
not often called for, because during the year of novitiate
a candidate to whom such things did not strongly appeal
would find this out and depart of his own accord. However, that there were some monks at Monte Cassino
excellent in other respects but weak in this, is suggested
by the Rule. This provided that monks who had little
taste for reading – which supposed about five hours a day
spent with a book – should be furnished with something
else to do, so that they might not waste their time.

Abbot Butler has worked out the monastic *horarium* in
Benedict's day. This varied according to the time of the
year, two in the morning being the ordinary time for
rising. Choir occupied the next hour and a half, after
which there was *meditatio* for an hour. This did not mean
meditation in our sense of the term but rather the reading
and the learning by heart of the psalms. From five to nine
there was the reading of devotional works, interrupted
only by Prime at six and concluding with Tierce. Then
there was work – whether in the fields or the kitchen or
the *scriptorium* – until about four, when the monks
gathered for None, with Vespers half an hour later and a
light meal at five, the day ending with Compline at six, so
that all retired to bed before the fading of the last light.

There seems to have been no daily Mass or Holy Communion at Monte Cassino except on Sundays and the major feasts of the Church. Abbot Butler therefore conjectures that what is called 'midnight office' – allowing monks to return to their beds for further sleep but involving a broken night – though it came to be the fashion, 'was not part of St Benedict's conception of the religious life'. There was no justification for it, for as the monks went to bed before the sun had completely set, they could rise early without any special fatigue. It might be added that, at least in summer, when the days were longer, there was a siesta in the middle of the day. All this indicates a simple life, frugal rather than austere. In place of the severe physical mortifications that had been taken for granted in the past, and which reappeared now and then for many centuries, an interior mortification was substituted, one far more salutary and meritorious. This was the conquest of self by obedience and graced by the humility which, even when not explicitly mentioned, entered into all the monk's actions.

It hardly needs to be said that the Benedictine ideal was not achieved by all Benedictines. It is clear from what is sometimes called the penal code of the Holy Rule that this is so. But also it is clear that a hope of correction through some form of penance was held: otherwise the refractory monk would simply have had to be summarily dismissed. Clearest of all is that the Rule was offered as a means of reaching Christian perfection. It is designed to reach it without undue strain, a perfection sought by a group in common, that very fact supplying opportunities for forbearance, patience and mutual charity.

Ten

Monks as Missionaries

THE ANCIENT monastic tradition had been expressed with the force so characteristic of him by St Jerome in the fourth century: 'The duty of a monk is not to teach but to weep.' Nor in the early days did the secular clergy do much preaching, this being regarded as something that appertained to the hierarchy, though it is obvious that only occasionally could a bishop, however zealous in this respect, have appeared in the pulpit of the many churches that were in his diocese. The time was to come, however, when at the Fourth Lateran Council, which met in 1215, the bishops were enjoined to appoint the preachers so badly needed by the faithful. Yet a century before this we had St Norbert founding the Premonstratensians, an order of canons, but thinking of his institute as for preachers, a role in which they must be said not to have been very successful, partly because they followed too closely the practices of the group of Benedictine monasteries known to us best under the title of Citeaux.

Early in the thirteenth century two mobile orders of friars made an almost simultaneous appearance with preaching as one of their objects. That founded by St Dominic was to be of priests, and priests who were picked men; that founded by St Francis of Assisi at first consisted mainly of laymen, who were by that very fact somewhat restricted in the subjects of which they were permitted to treat; so that repentance, not theology, was the theme of their exhortations. Both were called into being largely because of the crisis created by the Albigensian heresy – St Dominic's Order wholly so. He came to the rescue because some of the Cistercian abbots of southern France had failed in what they had tried to do. This was chiefly because they had gone out in abbatial state, with the result that the heretics simply refused to listen to any except men who lived in poverty. In the emergency – or just before it – various associations of laymen had taken upon themselves to preach, but tended themselves to drift toward heresy, and at least in the case of the Waldensians, being soon engulfed by it. This preaching, of course, was to a Europe that was supposedly Christian but in which the Church's teaching was imperfectly understood and still more imperfectly followed.

With all this the Benedictines had little to do, for their great missionary drive had long since been made, the monks afterward returning with a sigh of relief to the cloister which was for them their only true home. But the thirteenth-century effort of the friars needs to be mentioned, for their work supplemented what the Benedictines had done, or were to do again, since it is but natural for human nature to fall into recurrent spiritual declines.

There would have been little opening for the friars had Benedictine monks not preceded them, effecting the conversion of very wide tracts in Europe that were still pagan. In view of what they accomplished, this missionary work has to be looked upon as primarily a Benedictine enterprise. Yet there was no provision made for it in their Rule, which presupposed that the monks would keep within their abbeys and their adjacent fields. Not once do

we get the slightest indication that Benedict or his
followers, whether at Subiaco or Monte Cassino, went out
even to the people of the neighbourhood. The influence
they had was very considerable, we may be sure, but this
was exercised corporately by the good example they gave
and upon the stream of visitors they entertained. Quite
definitely they were not missionaries.

St Benedict had foretold that Monte Cassino would be
destroyed, as indeed happened about 589 at the hands of
the Lombards. He had also foretold that none of the
monks would be harmed. What he did not foretell was
that this disaster would prove providential. The settle-
ment they made in Rome led to their dispersal throughout
barbarian lands and opened a new chapter in Benedictine
history. Not only did this give a great impetus to the
general acceptance of the Rule by already existing monasteries, but under the Benedictine Pope Gregory the
Great, by the end of the sixth century the missionary
drive of the monks had already begun. Only to such a
well-organized and cohesive body could a work of this
enormous importance have been entrusted.

Gregory himself had wished that he could be a missionary to England and might have gone there had he not
been elected to the Chair of Peter. This, however, far
from diminishing his interest in the matter, gave him the
means for putting his plans all the more effectively into
action. The familiar story must be told again how, when
he saw some beautiful children being sold as slaves in the
Roman market and was informed that they were Angles,
he made his famous pun, *Non Angli sed angeli*. He knew, of
course, that there were already Christians in England, that
Irish monks had come into the north and into Wales and
had Christianized the people. He would also have heard

something, no doubt, about the work done by the same monks in Scotland. There were enough of them there to give their own name – that of the 'Scots' – to the land north of the Cheviot Hills and the river Tweed. But he also knew that in the south and centre of England everybody was pagan, and his heart went out to them. When he became Pope he was able to carry out his ideas; and thus his monks, or some of them, were transformed into missionaries. The conversion of most of western Europe stemmed from what was accomplished by them in England.

In 597 or thereabouts St Augustine (now known as of Canterbury) landed with his companions in Kent, the ground, fortunately, prepared for them by the circumstance that the local king had married a Christian wife, a Frankish princess. With that began the first Benedictine house outside of Italy. A claim has indeed been made for a prior foundation in Gaul, but the record of this is almost certainly fabulous, for it appears only in that life of St Maurus now considered to be an eighth-century forgery. It is almost certain there was no Benedictine monastery in France until a hundred years afterward, though it is not unlikely that the Benedictine Rule had been in part adopted by some of the monasteries there.

Yet even on the supposition that St Maurus had crossed the Alps, it was only to establish a monastery, not to be a missionary, for the land of the Franks was at least nominally Christian. One may say even more than this, for after the Merovingian Clovis (or, if one insists on being pedantic, Chlodwig) had accepted baptism at the hands of St Remi, his people turned from their Arianism to Catholic orthodoxy. Benedictines subsequently helped a good deal in consolidating these gains, but they had no part in initiating them.

To return to the mission of St Augustine, which was
where the missionary phase of Benedictine work began:
the extraordinary thing is how swiftly, effectually, and
completely the task of conversion was accomplished in
England. The abbey at Canterbury is not only the first of
such Benedictine establishments outside of Italy, but it
was the first of many such English abbeys. St Wilfrid,
though a monk of Lindisfarne, brought Ripon under the
Benedictine Rule in 660, and the twin monasteries of
Wearmouth and Jarrow were erected not long afterward,
the one in 674 and the other in 680, together with some
other houses of the same sort, mostly in the north. They
found their historian in the Venerable Bede, about whom
more will be said in a later chapter. From him we learn
that St Benet Biscop drew upon no less than seventeen
different religious rules, though that of St Benedict was
given the chief place. This eclecticism was also found in
some of the monasteries of France about the same time,
and was not at variance with St Benedict's idea that his
monks should take their spiritual good where they found
it. Yet, strictly speaking, St Benet Biscop could hardly
have been as eclectic as all that, for fully-formulated
monastic rules were rare. The reference must really be to
customs adopted by this or that individual monastery.
Even so, such houses usually may be considered Benedictine. In any event, it was not long before the Holy Rule
supplanted all others; it did so everywhere as soon as its
peculiar merits were fully understood.

Inevitably there were clashes between the Benedictine
missionaries to England and those (to use an anachronistic phrase for the sake of clarity) from Ireland and
Scotland. Ecclesiastical rivalry may have had something
to do with the matter; probably racial jealousies had more

weight. What also operated was a difference in discipline, though not a difference in doctrine (for there was none). The form of the tonsure became a bitterly fought issue; so also was the date at which Easter should be celebrated. It would seem that the Celtic missionaries were mainly at fault, for even so very gentle a person as Bede speaks with unwonted acrimoniousness when he touches upon their truculence.

Perhaps these differences could have been tolerated, for similar, and sometimes identical, differences are to be found in our own day in the usage of the Western Church and that of the various ancient Eastern groups in communion with Rome. But because of the quarrel that was allowed to develop, uniformity had to be imposed, though this was accomplished only by degrees. The upshot was not merely that the Roman Church eventually won a complete victory but that the culture of Rome prevailed – as the very structure of the English language attests.

Matthew Arnold discerns in the tone and colour of our Anglo-Saxon tongue something unmistakably Celtic, especially in its poetry, and he is right. Though the popular notion that the original Celtic inhabitants of the island were exterminated by the Teutonic invaders deserves a closer examination than can be given to it here, it is enough to call Bede as a witness that no such extermination occurred, for he constantly represents these exterminators as people who could only, with difficulty, maintain their own ground. But throughout England, except for Cornwall, where a Celtic language lingered on until the eighteenth century, and in Wales, where the indigenous language is still used, Anglo-Saxon came into being. It was a mere accident, having nothing whatever to do with any military conquest, but due only to the people who were taught in Anglo-Saxon by monks adopting that language as a matter of cultural convenience.

Occasionally, too, we find in early English monasticism an institution that would seem so strange now as to be impossible – that of the so-called 'double monastery', in which nuns and the brothers used the same church (it goes without saying at different hours of the day). This arrangement left the monks free for the work of conversion, while the nuns, as belonging to the 'practical sex', chose as their abbess one who took care of all the temporalities of the monastery. The redoubtable princess St Hilda ruled at Whitby in this way, and there were at one time in the adjoining house five monks who became bishops, not to mention Caedmon, who must be reckoned the earliest of English poets. It is amusing to read in Bede of Hilda's high-handed style in assigning Caedmon to his task, though this occurred only after the angel had visited the hitherto tongue-tied abbey serf.

The high degree of culture quickly reached by these barbarians as yet hardly dry from the baptismal font is attested in many ways, but especially by the achievement of the Venerable Bede, the only Englishman to be named a Doctor of the Church. (St Anselm does not count in this connection, though a profounder theologian than Bede, for he was a Norman importation.) We should never cease to dwell on the fact that Bede was born only seventy-six years after the arrival of St Augustine in Kent. There Augustine was succeeded as bishop by St Theodore, a Greek and the man who introduced Greek studies into England – a work continued by his own successor, Adrian of Canterbury. This is not intended to disparage in any way what was done so brilliantly for European culture by the learned Irish, for the lead in scholarship was once in their hands, and monks from Britain and elsewhere went to study in Ireland, in the same way as Irish monks, establishing themselves in Europe, made Irish scholarship so celebrated there. While the fruits of their learning were not lost, the Irish influence tended to decline with the spread of the Benedictine Rule, though this was adopted even by the Irish monks established in France in the sixth century by St Columbanus. It may be added that this decline was compensated for by a more co-hesive system than Irish individualism had been able to attain. While much that was valuable withered away, what was of more value to society at large came in to take its place.

Other great missionaries soon appeared, and most of them were offshoots of the work so grandly performed in England. Before the seventh century was out St Wilfrid was preaching to the Frisians, followed in 692 by St Willibrod and his twelve fellow monks. St Willibrod was made Bishop of Utrecht in 692, and lived in north-western Europe until his death in 738. Nor did this saint confine his activities to Frisia; though his attempt upon Denmark in the last year of the century was abortive, he won Thuringia, where he consecrated several churches, and in 721 and 725 was in Cleves and the territories beyond the Rhine. A Benedictine he was, though, like Wilfrid, he came from the abbey of Ripon, which was rather strongly marked by an Irish cast of thought. Irish individualism and brilliance were absorbed – perhaps to its own loss but to the strengthening of the Christendom now emerging – by the sobriety and steady industrious-ness of the paramount Benedictines.

Some other names of great Benedictine missionaries should be mentioned, though it should be understood that it is scarcely possible to do more than enumerate a few of the leaders in a group that always worked together. We have Swithbert in the Netherlands, Rupert and Emmeram in Austria, Adalbert in Bohemia, and Ansgar in Scandinavia. The work in the last named of these countries was immensely aided by King Olaf II (St Olaf), who in the eleventh century compelled his subjects to become Catholics, as he did also in Greenland and Iceland. In all of these he had the Faith inculcated by monks obtained from England, and without them nothing of permanent value could have been accomplished. We get a vivid picture of the veneration in which the holy King was held in the great medieval romances of Sigrid Undset. Although showing us how devout the Scandinavians were in the fourteenth century, she does not refrain from depicting their human frailties, somewhat to the scandal of some of her Catholic readers. To this day she is disparaged – by sections of the Catholic and non-Catholic public – though for opposite reasons: by the one she is regarded slightly askance for her frank admission that even the best of men and women may be sinners, especially by yielding to their passions; and by the other she is disparaged because she is so strongly religious. It becomes clear in her pages that Christ had to plough on stony and thorny ground, but that even upon such immalleable material He finally put His mark. The reasons why Christianity was later uprooted more thoroughly from Scandinavia than from any other part of Europe are not within the purview of this brief sketch.

Though not all of the missionary monks mentioned above were Englishmen, most of them were, and it must always be remembered that the effort was started by St Gregory when he sent St Augustine to Canterbury. Broadly, it may be said that the work of evangelization was accomplished, or at least put well under way, by the end of the tenth century – though King Olaf, of course, came later. Boso, the Benedictine Bishop of Merseburg, laboured among the Wends shortly before this time, but his work had to be renewed later by Vicelin, Bishop of Oldenburg, another Benedictine, during the first half of the twelfth century. All of which underlines the fact that a labour of this kind can never be considered as at an end, for those most heartily Christian, as in Scandinavia and in England itself, afterward fell suddenly into apostasy. When, later, England was saved from the fate that overtook the rugged peninsula of the north, the work was not to any great extent in Benedictine hands, but in those of the Jesuits and 'seminaries' trained under the future Cardinal Allen in the Low Countries, all of them ready for the martyrdom which in fact not a few of them had to suffer.

But even so passing a remark runs too far ahead, and is a matter of the general history of the Church rather than that of the Benedictines. To go back to our proper place, it must be said that the most illustrious of all Benedictine missionaries was St Boniface. The real name of this Englishman born at Crediton in Devonshire at the end of the seventh century was Winifrid, but Boniface was the name that Pope Gregory II gave him and by which he is now universally known. He had been a monk at Exeter and Winchester, and is one more instance of an English monk trained in a monasticism coloured by the Celtic mode. His work in Germany began in 719 and had, so to speak, three branches. He converted the wholly pagan Hessians and Saxons; he completed the conversion of the already partially Christianized Bavarians, Thuringians, and Franconians; and he organized, or reorganized,

ecclesiastical life among the Franks. This last was perhaps
not missionary work, strictly speaking, but it had to be
done if the gains made were to be retained, and it
demanded Boniface's powerful hand. Collaborating with
him were his nephews Willibald and Wunibald, and other
Benedictines who were not Englishmen, such as Pirmi-
nius, the founder of Reichenau; Gregory, who headed the
seminary at Utrecht; and Sturm, the founder of Fulda, to
this day the centre of Catholic Germany.

Fulda is an excellent example of what the Benedictines
meant to medieval society. The town itself, like so many
others, owes its very existence to the abbey established
there by Sturm in 744. This was largely because it
attracted so many learned men to its school of theological
studies, and had Alcuin, Rabanus Maurus (its abbot from
822 to 842), and Walafrid Strabo among its teachers.
Early in the tenth century it was strengthened and reformed by the arrival of new blood, this time monks from
Scotland, yet it again declined somewhat before the outbreak of the storm of the Reformation. In 968 its abbot
was made by the Pope the Primate of Germany and Gaul
and he subsequently ranked as a prince of the Empire, the
prince-bishopric being established again in 1752.

The subsequent history of Fulda need not concern us,
except that it should be remarked that from it usually
emanate the joint pronouncements of the German hierarchy. Though the original abbey and church have long
since gone, to be replaced by the present cathedral, Fulda
never forgets its sacred origins. Among its treasures is the
body of St Boniface, the Apostle of Germany, who, on
June 5, 755, was martyred with more than fifty others as
he was administering confirmation in the abbey church.
It is a wonder that he was borne with as patiently as he

was by a barbarian people, for he did not hesitate to sweep away much that they held dear. Utterly fearless, Boniface did such things as chop down trees sacred to the warrior god Thor, and was allowed to continue his missionary efforts only because those among whom he worked were awed by his courage and felt admiration for his holiness. The very fact that he so willingly accepted the risks that he did increased his prestige among a fierce race of sword swingers. At any rate, he was suffered long enough to establish Christianity firmly among them.

Through the monks in the Benedictine abbeys, especially those of England, certain people became not only Christian but learned in an incredibly short space of time, and to some extent they shed the light of their own culture through the districts in which they were centred. But to the majority of people in those days, when books were few and costly, and when there were fewer still who could read them, the Gospel had to go forth by word of mouth or by pictorial representations. Some of these converts may not have been able to learn much more than the fundamentals of the Faith and a few prayers, such as the *Paternoster* and the *Ave* and the *Kyrie Eleison*, and of course what their duties were as Christians, yet a good many also learned, if only by hearing them so constantly, the psalms of Sunday Vespers. And Mass was for all the shining centre of their Christian life. Even if the liturgy was acquired only in scraps, it must be said that everything in their lives was based upon the liturgical cycle. For these people Catholicism may be said to have worn a Benedictine aspect, yet the whole concern of the missionaries was to make good Christians, not to aggrandize themselves. Secular priests were as yet rare, but were welcomed when they began to arrive. The terms 'monk' and 'priest' were therefore practically identical in the people's minds. On such a foundation Catholicism, even when rather rudimentary, was solidly built.

In so far as was possible the monks established monasteries and not parishes. And when they founded the first parishes most of them were near the abbey so they could be served by monks from the central house. In cases where these churches were so far away as to require a priest to be resident among his flock in the parish house, such dependencies of the abbey tended to become priories in which a full monastic life could be observed. (We can see today a very similar tendency operating in the Benedictine parishes of the United States; it is always a sign of healthy Benedictine life.)

The same tendency may be observed in the late Middle Ages. While now and then monks were called upon to serve in diplomatic or political capacities, or sometimes as private chaplains, tasks of this sort usually were taken over by the secular clergy, into whose field of activities such things more naturally fell. And when a monk was made a bishop, he was ordinarily given a see where a priory was attached to the cathedral; there the monks chanted the Office, as should be done in every cathedral but which in our own time rarely happens. Westminster Cathedral is an exception, but there the choral obligations are fulfilled by minor canons who are secular priests. Obviously such duties are far better performed by Benedictines than by any other class of the clergy. Westminster Cathedral might now be said almost to replace Westminster Abbey, whose monks dispersed by Henry VIII and briefly restored by Queen Mary were at last finally silenced by Elizabeth. 'Bare ruined choirs, where late the sweet birds sang.'

As has been several times stressed, what Benedictines

undertake is a corporate effort, not the performance of an individual, however gifted. While it would be too much to claim that no vain or ambitious men have appeared among the monks, at least it may be said that it is rather hard for them to find scope for their personal brilliance within the monastic framework. As Montalembert pointed out in his *Monks of the West*: 'It is in the cloister and in the bosom of the sanctuary, where they passed their lives, that the monks have exercised the power of attraction which has drawn to them the entire world. The whole Church has, in a manner, established itself upon the monastic order, draws from it its spirit of virtue, and comes to renew in men's souls the worship and respect due to God.' Normally their work is carried out in the monastery, but in exceptional situations Benedictine life has repeatedly shown elasticity enough to adapt itself to any circumstances that have to be met without in the least losing its distinctive character. Never was this more true than during its missionary drive in the early Middle Ages. It was through this that most of the pagan nations of Europe were brought into the Church. They were secured all the more firmly because the great work initiated by Gregory the Great when he sent monks to England was performed so quietly, with a minimum of publicity, and no flourish at all.

Eleven

Sketch of Benedictine History

THE TITLE of this chapter would be misleading if it led anyone to expect even the smallest of capsule histories of the Benedictine Order. To make the matter clear at once, it should be explained that all I have in mind is the presentation of some aspects of what happened to the Benedictine monks during the Middle Ages. It should perhaps, be added here that neither in this historical section nor in any of the other chapters of the book is pretence made of giving information that is other than fragmentary.

To a considerable extent the fortunes of the Benedictines have gone along the lines of those of the Church itself, which means that good periods have been followed by bad, though always with the power of renewal. Of course the Benedictines arrived too late on the scene to have suffered anything like the persecution endured by the early Christians, though here and there they have provided martyrs. When Monte Cassino was sacked and destroyed by the Lombards toward the end of the seventh century, the monks succeeded in escaping personal injury; indeed the act of vandalism which obliged them to seek a refuge in Rome, as we have seen, even proved providential, as it put them in position for their missionary enterprises Subsequently they suffered ruthless spoliation and even suppression in several countries. The worst of these experiences occurred at the time of the Protestant Reformation and during the Napoleonic hegemony. But there was also the subtler, slower, and more prolonged form of spoliation under the *in commendam* system introduced in several Catholic countries, whereby lay abbots, or clerics not members of the community, were empowered to appropriate the larger part of the monastic revenues, leaving to the monks themselves only a pittance for their support.

In addition to these external assaults there were periods of some degree of internal decline, and these sometimes occurred when the abbeys appeared in a very flourishing condition – sometimes perhaps because of that very reason. This may be, however, and often has been, exaggerated, almost always by those who wanted to get hot, greedy hands upon the loot. Though it may be true that a particular abbey, or group of abbeys, became lax, there was always an effort at recovery and reform that set things to rights again, that is, when the monasteries were not forcibly suppressed. Much more often we find that any decline in monastic fervour was due to pressure and not on account of anything for which the monks themselves can be held responsible. Broadly Dr Johnson's view was justified: he said that whenever he heard of a monastery he felt that he wanted to kiss the ground.

The law always seemed to operate that when a monastery was poor, it was regarded as a burden; when it was rich, it offered a temptation to the powerful. The same kind of people who complained of having to support a religious class, suggesting that this class of men had vowed themselves to poverty in order to escape work, swung round indignantly when quiet industriousness made them prosperous, to complain about the rich monks (or those whom they imagined to be rich); they regarded themselves as doing something praiseworthy in reducing them to a poverty more consonant with the monastic state. That the despoilers vastly augmented their own wealth was (by them) thought only fitting: they had wives and children to maintain, and also a private army of retainers to pay to protect their possessions against rivals who might become marauders.

The first phase of lay domination over the monasteries came rather soon after the acceptance of the Benedictine Rule throughout the empire of Charlemagne and his immediate successor. However, as late as 818 most of the Breton monasteries continued to hold on to the Irish usages, but at that date Louis the Fair compelled them to accept uniformity. This forcible imposition of the Benedictine Rule as the only one permitted to monks no doubt had some advantages but also some serious drawbacks. The first was that St Benedict of Aniane who was so largely instrumental in imposing it, and who naturally congratulated himself upon what he had done, introduced a rigidity foreign to the spirit of the first St Benedict whose Rule had allowed a wide latitude to the discretion of the individual abbot. But under his namesake of Aniane virtually no discretionary powers were permitted: to the smallest detail every monastery had to be like all the rest.

The price paid for this adoption of the Rule throughout the empire was very high and of a kind never envisaged. The civil authorities soon came to consider that they had rights of control. Worse still, those who protected the monasteries came to believe that they owned them. This meant that they quartered themselves with their wives and children (occasionally even their mistresses) in a wing – always the best wing – of the monastery buildings. It is hardly necessary to say that this resulted in a grave disruption of monastic life. The depressing story is related in the first volume of Dom Philibert Schmitz's *Histoire de l'Ordre de Saint-Benoît*. It need not be gone into any further here.

Another factor that operated was that the abbeys, even when they managed to free themselves of this evil, tended to become part of the feudal system. As Schmitz put it: 'The abbey possessed henceforth all the rights of a feudal lordship; it also had to shoulder its obligations.' The abbots were indeed exempted from the duty of leading their tenants in war – though now and then we hear of their actually donning armour, even if they themselves struck no blow – but always they were expected to raise their quota of men at arms at the demand of their feudal overlord.

That was one part of the matter. Another was (to take England by way of example) that the abbots, or a certain number of them, had seats in the House of Lords together with the bench of bishops. And in medieval times the House of Lords had immense legislative powers – powers that in our own day have been reduced to nothingness so that the Upper House seems to be kept for hardly more than decorative effect. Nevertheless, we do not find that the abbots in medieval England regularly exercised their rights. They did not do so because they were not political personages, and usually attended Parliament only when questions directly affecting the ecclesiastical order were under discussion. Even then they were sometimes politely 'excused' by a royal order which it was understood must be obeyed. It was so, at all events when Henry VIII was preparing his monastic 'reforms'. A few abbots who had been persuaded that the expropriation of the smaller monasteries would be for the strengthening of the large abbeys over which they ruled were graciously permitted to be present, as they could be trusted to vote the right way; but the others were met on the road by a messenger with a letter from the King in which he kindly explained that, out of his consideration for age and infirmity, they need not make this difficult journey. Those who were wise took the hint. In other parts of Europe, especially the empire, abbatial grandeur prevailed, some prelates ranking as prince-bishops. But in all cases these glorious magnates actually existed on sufferance; those holding the real control were the great nobles, and sometimes the king.

Abbot Bulter sets the medieval period of monasticism as existing from the Fourth Council of the Lateran (1215) to the Council of Constance (1418). But this strikes me as rather arbitrary, especially as it makes 800 to 1215 the period of lay domination, whereas it might be more correct to say that, while the form of domination changed, the domination itself did not, in spite of the grandeur which was allowed to appear. However, this probably is no more misleading than are most of such divisions in history, for while certain dates do mark epochs, we usually have to expect little more than a transformation, the gliding of one period into another. Often the most fitting epigraph is: The more things change, the more they remain the same. Yet Butler is undoubtedly right when he declares: 'The medieval abbot ... was really great, and no doubt he worked great good for Church and State alike. But he was not, he could not be, St Benedict's abbot.' He was too much of a territorial magnate for that.

Let us again consider the case of England. When Henry IV was King it was seriously proposed in Parliament that, if only the surplus wealth of the Church were confiscated, and of course put to better use, enough money would be obtained to endow fifteen new earls, fifteen hundred new knights, over six thousand squires, and still leave the King £20,000 a year for himself. Forty thousand priests were to be left, each with a living of seven marks a year. Sir John Oldcastle's fantastic suggestions were exposed for the ridiculous nonsense that they were.

The notion nevertheless persisted and in 1528 Simon Fish published his *Supplication for Beggars*, in which he wanted the wealth of the Church used for public purposes. He also had a set of statistics to prove his point. Estimating that there were 52,000 parishes in England, averaging ten households, he supposed that it could be said that each of these households gave a penny every quarter to the friars, by which method he reached the conclusion that in this way the friars obtained an annual income of £436,333 6s 8d from this source alone. Yet, he added, this was only what the friars managed to extract; the Church generally, that is the abbeys and the bishoprics and the better livings, had half the manorial holdings of England in their possession. How absurd this all was appeared when the monasteries were suppressed: then it was discovered that their yearly rentals brought in only £320,280 10s 0d, which indeed was a lot of money but it represented only about a fifth of the country's manorial holdings, very far from our poor Fish's half.

Other matters have to be considered. In the true Middle Ages England was fortunately without commendatory abbots, except for Cardinal Wolsey's being the titular of the abbey of St Albans. Yet great as monastic wealth appeared to be on paper, and great as it sometimes was in fact, many monasteries, when accepting large endowments, undertook to see to it that any descendants of the donors who came down in the world would be supported

as permanent guests of the houses to which these endowments had been made. Such guests expected the best of
everything, and like annuitants lived on and on. To this
it must be added that the crown every now and then
ordered a monastery to pay a pension that should have
come out of the royal exchequer. All in all, because of
these and other drains upon their resources, the wealth
of the monasteries, though still often very considerable,
was nothing like so large as people imagined.

More will be said a little later about monastic expro-
priations, but first it might be as well to glance at some of
the attempts made by the monasteries themselves to check
lay encroachment. Thus the Cluniac and similar reforms,
though at wide variance in their centralization from the
original Benedictine idea that each house should be autonomous – for under Cluny there were several hundreds
of dependencies – at least did free these monasteries from
the commendatory system. This was accomplished by
making them subject only to the Holy See. St Benedict
of Aniane had anticipated the centralization, becoming,
in effect, the general of a religious Order, yet he had most
unfortunately opened the door to lay intrusions. Cluny
discovered a way of closing that door again, and very
securely. Yet again the ideal was defeated. It was Cardinal
Newman who saw into the heart of the matter when he
described Benedictinism as 'an organization, diverse,
complex, and irregular, and variously ramified, rich rather
than symmetrical, with many origins and centres and new
beginnings, and the action of local influence. . . . Instead
of proceeding on plan and system, and from the will of a
superior, it has shot forth and run out as if spontaneously,
and has shaped itself according to events, from an irresist-
ible fullness of life within, and from the energetic self-

action of the parts, like those symbolical creatures in the prophet's vision which went every one of them straight-forward, whither the impulse of the Spirit was to go.' This was at all events the Benedictine concept, and it has shaped most of Benedictine history, though now and then there was rather too much yielding to 'the action of local influences', in the sense of too much external domination.

Even when the later medieval abbeys were free to re-turn to their origins, had they only chosen to do so, a tradition of magnificence had been built up, if merely because of the need for resisting the encroachment of king and nobles. Mr Workman, a Protestant, who is the author of a valuble work under the title of *The Evolution of the Monastic Ideal*, may assert too much in saying, despite the sympathy and fairness he generally shows, that a monas-tery became 'a club of celibate landlords under a rule', yet there is much to justify the witticism. We know that even the Carmelite nuns of St Teresa's sixteenth-century convent, the Encarnación, while they were all women of excellent character, developed a good deal of worldliness. They had beautifully furnished apartments and were free to receive an unlimited number of visitors in the convent parlour and to make visits to their families. The punctilio of rank was insisted upon, and if the convent fare was sometimes meagre, this was not because austerity was de-sired but because the Encarnación, though socially very select, was not very wealthy. Similarly we find St Vincent de Paul, when serving on the Council of Conscience, being greatly shocked at what he calls the 'scandalous lives' of a group of nuns who came under his jurisdiction. Yet it turns out that his judgment was not according to ordinary standards but what he considered to be seemly in a religious. 'There are several nuns,' he writes of a group

who had come to Paris to escape the dangers of the
Fronde, 'who are not modest in their attire and, in the
parlour wear gloves, combs with rosettes of ribbons, or
scarlet-coloured streamers, and gold watches and, when
reprimanded for doing so by the Abbess, said the Father
Provincial had given them permission.' There was, after
all, nothing so very terrible in that, even if it does not
quite fit in with what one expects of religious.

In the same way in fourteenth-century England one
finds Chaucer depicting his Prioress – obviously a very
good woman, despite her little affectations – sporting a
brooch and keeping pet dogs, not observing the Benedictine Rule as she should, though a pious and a charming
person. He lets her down much more lightly than he does
his monk (also clearly a Benedictine), though even that
gentleman was worldly rather than wicked. His habit
sleeves were furred against the cold; a fat swan was his
favourite roast; and 'full many a dainty horse had he in
stable'. But he was 'a manly man, to be an abbot able',
yet he was then only the 'keeper of a cell' or the superior
of a small dependent house. With his casual Catholic
satire Chaucer explains that his monk found 'the Rule of
Seint Maur or Seint Beneit' rather 'streit', and so made
no great effort to observe it very carefully.

> How shall the world be served?
> Let Austin have his swink to him reserved.

In other words, let the monastic legislators keep their
own religious rules; the monks of the fourteenth century
were not going to incommode themselves.

The Chaucerian pictures, though they bear every evidence of being very true to life, do not necessarily mean
that all Benedictines were like the Monk of his Pilgrims,

or the Prioress; but there must have been enough of such people to permit their introduction. At least they were a good deal better in every way than some of the ecclesiastical hangers-on he shows us. Abbot Bulter's remark, even if not made with this sort of thing in mind, applies closely enough to be quoted: 'It is by common consent recognized that, on the whole and in its great currents, Benedictine history has been true to the idea of the Founder, a legitimate development, not a perversion.' Even during what may be thought of as periods of decline, there have always been monasteries, and a large number of individual monks and nuns who retained the Benedictine spirit undimmed and who, as soon as the chance occurred, brought it again into general acceptance.

The trouble lay largely in the fact that during the true Middle Ages the monasteries were obliged to live within the framework of society as it was at the time. As Schmitz writes: 'All these prerogatives unfortunately involved the monks in the affairs of the world. These came close to secularizing the abbey.' That fact is unfortunate; but against it must be put another fact: a tendency, even though strong, remained no more than a tendency. That the 'club of celibate landlords' lived under the Benedictine Rule, meant, even when they observed that Rule somewhat negligently, that they observed it well enough to remain monks, a class of men set apart, not only from the laity but from the secular clergy.

After all, in England the monasticism we see during the Middle Ages was, even at its most lax (and it was never very lax), far superior to conditions during the depredations of the Danes. In many places during that period a regular monastic life was impossible. However, Cardinal Gasquet, who wrote a good deal on such

matters, declares that it is a false assumption that this life
'was practically extinct in England during the early days of
the tenth century, surviving only in a few old men, who
mumbled their matins in Glastonbury.' The name of St
Dunstan – scholar, lover of song, metalworker, so much
of a scientist as to be accused of practising the black arts,
and, above all, a monastic reformer – is enough to prove
that Benedictinism in the England of the tenth century
had immense vitality. Yet it can be granted that English
monks did need some revivification, and when this was
brought about it was largely a foreign importation,
in the sense of being made by Englishmen who had received their training abroad. And of course the rather
sluggish current of English life was enormously quickened
after the Norman conquest, which was much to the bene-
fit of monasticism as well as to other aspects of that society.

To give some figures that may serve to indicate how
flourishing was medieval Benedictinism: Corbie at one
time had three hundred and fifty monks, St Wandrille
three hundred, and one document attributes nine hundred
to Jumièges. Fifty or sixty was a common number, and
Canterbury had about a hundred and fifty, Gloucester a
hundred, and Abingdon and Westminster eighty each.
Cluny in its heyday had four hundred monks in the
abbey, and while the figures for Jumièges may be exaggerated (as one feels must be the case) to govern even a
hundred monks would raise a number of administrative
problems. Thomas Carlyle, no friend to the monastic
system, nevertheless used the masterful Abbot Samson of
St Edmundsbury (drawing freely upon the chronicle left
by Jocelin of Brakelond) to pit the splendid past against a
squalid Victorian England. The tenants of that monastic
landlord, he discovered, much to his surprise, honoured,

loved, and admired him.' As for monks in general, though he considered them completely outmoded, he is constrained to say of them handsomely and truly: 'Religion lies over them like an all-embracing heavenly canopy, which is not spoken of, which in all things is presupposed without speech.'

Yet Henry VIII completely uprooted the English monasteries, something that had been prepared for by the Black Death, though it is not being suggested that it would not have happened in any event. But what must be remembered is that the Black Death worked havoc among the monks, as among all classes of people, so that in some monasteries every member of the community succumbed to the pestilence. In all communities the number of fatalities was so great as to make it impossible for the survivors to carry out their religious duties as well as formerly. Bishops, in order to meet the emergency, ordained men for the secular priesthood who had hardly any other qualifications than that they were able to memorize enough Latin to say Mass and administer the Sacraments. This last situation carried down to the sixteenth century, so that St Thomas More had to point out that a crying evil of the time was that there were too many priests – so many that a sizable proportion of them were engaged in what were not really clerical functions, but were acting as tutors or stewards in the houses of the nobility (though usually with the title of chaplain), and because of their priestly inadequacy gave a handle to the reformers. (He, too, of course, wished for reform, though of a different kind from the one beginning to be advocated.)

In the case of the monasteries the result was often that they had too few monks, and that although their holdings in land were intact, in many instances they were unable to manage their estates very efficiently. A reorganization was called for. When St John Fisher was Chancellor of Cambridge University he was permitted to suppress several religious establishments that had ceased to serve any very useful purpose; so after placing their inmates in other convents, he was free to take their revenues for the support of a college. Cardinal Wolsey, also with papal permission, suppressed a much larger number, though one may doubt whether his motive was not so much th glory of God as the glory of Wolsey who planned colleges at Oxford and Ipswich, his home town. The principle of suppressing rundown houses to obtain funds for a better purpose was sound enough.

Unfortunately all this gave to Wolsey's main agent in the matter, Thomas Cromwell, a training and ideas that were destined – after Henry's breach with the Holy See – to involve all the English monasteries in ruin. The first stage followed the Wolseyan lines: only the smaller monasteries were to be suppressed, those with fewer than twelve monks or nuns. Twelve was not unreasonably considered to be the minimum required for the solemn chanting of the Divine Office. Less reasonably there was also brought in a yardstick of £200 a year in revenues. Those who had less were accused of abominable iniquity, unless they contrived to prove their virtue by bribing Cromwell.

In the end, however, it was found that even the most famous of monasteries – those praised for their mode of life by the act of 1536 – were as wicked as their smaller and helpless fellows. The abbots who surrendered gracefully were handsomely pensioned; so also, in a small way, were such of the religious as could be persuaded to bring charges against the moral conditions of the house. But abbots who were stubborn were hanged, and monks or nuns who were unco-operative were simply turned adrift. In any event, the result came to much the same thing as far as the monasteries as institutions were concerned: while individual religious were sometimes well provided for, the monasteries were destroyed.

This does not mean that the actual fabrics were obliterated, for when useful for some secular purpose they were put to use. But in many cases even those in cities narrowly escaped destruction, as when Protector Somerset, during Edward VI's reign, was within an inch of pulling down Westminster Abbey itself to use stones with which to build his London palace. Still these people were mainly interested in the land of the estates, rather than any building upon it. By one means or another the new rich acquired most of the wealth that had, theoretically, been appropriated for the enrichment of the crown, for what the king himself got went down a rat hole so fast that both Henry and young Edward were obliged to debase the coinage, and leave a number of unpaid debts. It was not until the much-maligned Mary Tudor came to the throne that any effort at public honesty was attempted. She, good, conscientious woman, returned to the Church the £60,000 a year still left, and refounded a number of religious houses during her brief, unhappy reign. But it should be noted that she was powerless to bring about England's reconciliation with the Holy See until explicit guarantees had been given that those who had plundered the monasteries would not be expected to disgorge. So nervous were the brigands that even when England again had a Catholic king, James II, he found it advisable to have his Benedictine chaplain offer assurances that there was no thought of obliging them to restore what had been looted from the monks.

Though the monasteries themselves all went down in

England, there was not the total conquest of Catholicism
that marks the history of Scandinavia. This was largely
because a most heroic band of missionaries arrived from
abroad – Jesuits and men trained in Dr Allen's seminaries – who went about in disguise, so keeping alive the
Faith in the hearts of many people. Benedictines had
little to do with this, though one should not forget the
Benedictine Father Barkworth who, when just about to
be hanged, drawn, and quartered, was admonished by a
Protestant minister at the gibbet to remember that Christ
died for him. 'And so do I for Christ' was Barkworth's
magnificent rejoinder. Furthermore, we should always
remember the two missionaries who, upon their arrival
from abroad, discovered an old man named Sigebert
Buckley, who had been a monk of Westminster Abbey
during its brief restoration under Mary. He conferred the
Benedictine habit on them; then, after their year of novitiate, they took their vows in Father Buckley's presence
on the feast of the Presentation, November 21, 1607. As
there was no possibility of re-establishing the full Benedictine life in England, they did so on the Continent; but
at least this meant that the Benedictine line was not
altogether broken. When at last the monks were free to
return to England they could say that they had had a
continuous history, one that reached back to the arrival
of St Augustine at Canterbury in 597.

In the Protestant parts of Germany the methods employed were relatively mild, but this was because the
resistance was less heroic. At Bursfeld, for example, the
abbot and all the monks willingly accepted the Reform,
after which they were left undisturbed as a community.
Yet after a Catholic prince obtained the reins of government some years later, the same abbot of Bursfeld was one

of the first to come back to the Church. Dom Schmitz in the third volume of his *Histoire* gives a further account of conditions. At Clus, the abbot remained faithful among a community that had accepted Lutheranism. At Naumburg, though the abbot married, at least two of his monks remained Catholics. At Hillersleben the monks asked that their abbot, 'who had been called to the good estate of marriage', be permitted to remain in command. The prior of Schlüchtern married but continued to be a member of the community. It was all a bit confusing and more than a bit amusing, but it must be admitted to have made subsequent restoration not too difficult.

So, also, there was something to be said for the system of partial expropriation known as *in commendam*. If it had been adopted in England it might have made it feasible for the monasteries to continue, though in a weakened state. Yet one may be glad that it was not in vogue there. In France it saved the abbeys from the worst blasts of the storm; however, in Scotland it saved nothing. There it had been introduced in order to set aside a source of income for royal bastards, which only added to the scandal and to the fury of such men as John Knox. In France things had never been so bad as that, though they were bad enough. There it was merely a means of supporting the *protégés* of powerfully placed people. Even Vincent de Paul as a young man – not yet a saint but soon to become one – was glad to obtain the *commendam* of the Cistercian Abbey of Saint-Léonard-de-Chaumes. The system was so very general that to this day the title in France for a secular priest is *abbé*, those in religion being addressed as *père*. Pecuniary reasons for turning Protestant hardly applied when Catholic families could obtain without any upheaval a share of the monastic wealth.

Though only too often such 'abbots' lived and dressed as fashionable men of the world, it did also happen that now and then a commendatory abbot would enter the community to which he was appointed and become an edifying monk. It was so to a terrifying degree with the Abbé Armand Jean de Bouthillier de Rancé who in 1664, when he was nearing forty, proceeded to overhaul his Cistercians, with so high a hand. He got at loggerheads with many of the religious of his time, especially the Benedictines of both the Black and White species. It is clear why he obtained from Brémond the title of the 'Thundering Abbot'. There is no denying that he knew his own censorious mind and performed an enduring work, though one notices that present-day Trappists prefer to be known as the Cistercians of the Strict Observance. But his case was so striking and extreme that it will have to be treated in the next chapter. We have here a man of so forceful a personality that he could steal the show if that were permitted. The readers of this book will therefore have to be content to see him merely touched upon in connection with a number of later modifications of the Benedictine idea.

Twelve

Development and Divergencies

Development, it has been pointed out, was allowed for by St Benedict in the Holy Rule, though he could not have foreseen the lines that it has sometimes taken. The abbot was given wide discretionary powers, and each community or group of communities – those known as congregations – while seeing to it that each abbey remained autonomous, have found it necessary to introduce constitutions in order to further the monastic life as seemed desirable in a particular time or place. As the modifications introduced have been so many and various, it may usually be sufficient to indicate that they did occur; indeed, it would be impossible to do more in a book of this narrow scope.

There are, however, some developments that demand fuller mention, as they went beyond what we see in the constitutions of modern congregations, and represent something more fundamental. When at the beginning of the ninth century St Benedict of Aniane, strongly backed by Charlemagne, succeeded in imposing the Rule throughout the Western empire, he also sought to impose absolute uniformity everywhere, and to transform the monks into a religious Order, in the modern sense, with himself as general. That part of it did not last, except as this reorganization might be regarded as an anticipation of the Cluniac reform. But it did bring about sweeping changes, for a certain degree of eclecticism had been common in monasteries which we rightly consider Benedictine. This was no longer tolerated.

Again it must be stressed that the whole idea of a general is totally at variance with the Benedictine spirit. While now the various congregations of abbeys have an abbot who presides when the abbots meet, he has no jurisdiction over them. Thus the Archabbot of St Vincent's is merely the head of the first Benedictine house founded in the United States, and though St Meinrad's in Indiana is now also an archabbey, this also is merely a titular honour. As for the Abbot Primate in Rome, whose office has existed only about sixty years, his duties definitely do not include any direction of the Benedictine Order; in fact, it is questionable whether the Benedictines constitute an Order at all. More will be said about the Primate a little later.

In general it may be said that though groups of Benedictines have come into existence who give their own interpretation to the Rule (as they are perfectly free to do) and may even adopt a distinctive name and a habit different from that worn by the main body of 'Black Monks', no such divisions have occurred as have several times troubled Franciscan history. While it is true that the mode of life adopted by some Benedictine groups makes them very unlike the main body of their brethren, there is no breaking away, for what is there to break away from? These groups may modify even the traditional degree of moderate austerity, or may claim to be observing the Rule with special strictness, and sometimes there has been among Benedictines a good deal of controversy regarding this or that point, but formal severance in their case is rather hard to imagine. All at least comply with what

Cardinal Gasquet has to say of the difference between a monasticism of this type and a religious Order: the monk enters an abbey with no other purpose than to arrive at perfection just by being a good monk, whereas a member of a religious Order – though of course he also aims at perfection – is well aware that the Order he has joined engages in a particular activity, or a number of activities, to any one of which he may be assigned by his superiors. Usually he joins in expectation (or hope) of being given a particular work to do. The Benedictine, on the other hand, enters a family, and the abbot is his father rather than his superior. The abbey he enters is his home for life, and he cannot be sent elsewhere except by his own consent. Nor, for that matter, is he free to leave it to engage in some external work that has attracted his fancy. Stability naturally cuts both ways.

Following the centralizing effort made by St Benedict of Aniane in the early ninth century – and very largely as a consequence – we have seen how the powerful of the world, who were supposed to be the protectors of monasticism came during the next century to be its exploiters. We accordingly had the *in commendam* system in its crudest form, without any of the refinements and disguises that later came to surround it. It was some time before such an incubus was sloughed off.

The Cluniac reform which began in the tenth century and gathered strength until the twelfth, after which time it gradually lost ground, was, among other things, an effort to check these scandals. As such it succeeded, for Cluny and all the very large number of its dependencies – which were to be found in several countries, though mostly in France – contrived to place themselves directly under the Pope himself, so as to be exempt from ordinary

episcopal control, and still more from any lay interference. It decisively broke the shackles under which
monasticism had lain, yet Cluny succeeded only at the
heavy price of a centralization that was not Benedictine.
The dependencies, many of which were large and important enough to become autonomous abbeys, nevertheless
remained merely priories, whose superiors were appointed by the abbot of Cluny. In fact, many an abbey was
only too glad to reduce its own status and to become a
priory, so as to come within the Cluniac orbit where it
would be safe. As they could not be plundered, they
inevitably grew wealthy, and that, too, was an induce-
ment to many a Benedictine house to seek such an
affiliation. But it was not so much that they wished to
become rich as that they sought to escape being robbed.

This is not to suggest that the Cluniac houses were
luxurious, for splendid as they often were structually, the
life lived in them was austere. But factors at flat variance
with the Benedictine concept manifested themselves.
One was that the monks did virtually none of the manual
work prescribed by the Rule, not because they were
lazy but because they were much too busy in another
way. The magnificence of the Cluniac churches inevitably
suggested to the monks that the Divine Office should
be rendered in them with the highest degree of solemnity.
The ordinary performance of the Office was not nearly
enough in their eyes, for even when this was chanted
slowly with some embellishments, it could only be
slightly lengthened. Therefore, a daily singing of the
Office for the Dead and the Little Office, not to mention
some new-fangled liturgical devices, were added until
the Cluniac monks spent almost the entire day in choir.
Indeed, in order to augment the number of choir monks

– again with the intention of making the services more splendid – the novitiate that St Benedict had introduced was so abbreviated as to become practically nonexistent. Choir monks were rapidly secured by this method – though one might have thought they were already numerous enough – and while the Cluniac chant was almost unbelievably grand, another result was that in the Cluniac organization not a few monks were professed who were eventually to discover they had no vocation for the monastic state.

Gasquet points out the weakness of the system, a weakness inherent in the very real glory of Cluny. The Benedictine concept of the family life was undermined, for most of the Cluniac monks never saw Cluny, though they were professed for that abbey and their vows were taken in the name of its abbot. Gasquet adds: 'The greatness of Cluny was kept up in a fictitious way, and if for a time the means adopted sustained the great edifice, it only resulted in more complete ruin when the collapse came.' In other words, the success of Cluny was the cause of its eventual undoing. Its famous abbot, Peter the Venerable, was able to summon a chapter of several hundred priors, but they had departed from Benedictine simplicity and had obtained their emancipation from lay interference – something of course in itself very much to be desired – only by constituting themselves a religious Order of the most rigid kind.

A reaction against the magnificence of Cluny occurred with the founding of Citeaux and its group of abbeys. It was founded in 1098 by St Robert, who was succeeded by St Alberic and then by the Englishman, St Stephen Harding. But it owed most of its prestige to that extraordinary genius St Bernard, who joined with his brothers and who

even persuaded his married sister to take the veil. Young
as Bernard was, he became abbot of Clairvaux and one of
the most celebrated preachers and theologians the Church
has ever produced, for which services he has obtained the
very rare honour of being named a Doctor of the Church.
Yet he was so frequently engaged in affairs that took him
away for long periods, and even when at home conducted
so voluminous a correspondence, that one cannot but wonder how he was able to have any leisure for contemplation,
except for the fact that we know from his writings that he
was among the very greatest masters of the spiritual life.

What matters here, though, is not St Bernard's multi-
farious activities but what he accomplished in the way of
building up Citeaux. This group, while retaining, as Cluny
did not, the concept that each abbey was autonomous –
and Bernard founded more than a hundred and fifty religious houses – nevertheless conferred on the abbot of
Citeaux such powers as turned him for all intents and purposes into a general. Stephen Harding made it perfectly
plain that 'all monks in the confederation [were] to observe
the Rule of St Benedict in all things as it is observed in
the New Monastery'. This means that the Cistercians
gave a somewhat novel interpretation of the Holy Rule
and intended to impose this rigorously. It could, of
course, be argued (and was) that no novelties were introduced, but that what Citeaux was really doing was to
abolish all mitigations that had crept in – particularly
regarding food and silence – and that they were returning
to the primitive observance. As against this it may be
argued, with equal plausibility, that the Black Benedictines, even when not keeping the letter of the law, were
more faithful to its spirit. Dietary regulations that were
appropriate for Italy were not so appropriate for colder

climates. And while St Benedict enjoined silence as the ordinary practice of monks, it is clear from several passages of the Rule that he did not intend silence to be absolute. Citeaux, unlike Cluny, did try to return to Benedictine simplicity, both in its buildings and its services, and the abbot really was the father of his monks, even if he was subject to the abbot of Citeaux. Yet even more than Cluny, Citeaux instituted a uniformity and a system of government that can only be said to have transformed the monasteries of its group into a religious Order. And while all this may have worked for efficiency, and have served to check the *in commendam* evil, again one must say what was gained was accompanied by loss, and that Citeaux, like Cluny, which was so different from it in many respects, sacrificed a great deal that Benedictines hold dear.

The colour of the habit worn by Cistercians – which was white, as was that of the Olivetans founded in the thirteenth century, while that of the Sylvestrians of the twelfth century was blue – was not important, for one must infer from the words of the Rule that it was a matter about which Benedict was indifferent. It was rather more momentous that the Camaldolese and the Vallombrosians should tend toward the eremitical rather than the cenobitic life, even though that, too, seems to be allowed for as a possibility by the Rule. At least it has to be said of both Cluny and Citeaux that they sought to produce monks living in community rather than solitaries. Both also laid a good deal of emphasis on a rigorous plainness of fare, but where Cluny went in for great splendour in its churches, Citeaux kept its edifices bare, unadorned, and harked back to what one might anachronistically call 'puritanism'. It would not permit any ornaments in its churches except crucifixes of wood; the candlesticks must be of iron, the censers of brass, and the chalices themselves were to be not of gold but only of silver gilt. Mr Workman, on the basis of the fact that Citeaux did not encourage the use of rhyme in its hymns, decides that St Bernard cannot be the author of the famous hymn always attributed to him, the *Jesu, dulcis memoria*.

With regard to this last, I am willing to concede that he is right, though not necessarily on the basis of his own argument, for people are not always very consistent. According to a very circumstantial story St Bernard, while preaching the crusade in the Rhine Valley, added to the *Salve* in an access of fervour the rhyming couplet which is now its close: *O clemens, o pia, O dulcis virgo Maria*. There have been some who have thought that this ruined the prayer; others have vastly admired it. While my own feeling is that the *Salve* might have dispensed with that rhyme, I also think that the plain chant in which it is sung has reached a conclusion of great – almost excessive – beauty. St Bernard's rhyming close may or may not be called for, but after the musician had worked it in, making of it a series of jewels, those may have the best of the argument who consider it the loveliest passage of Christian music. Huysmans even went so far as to declare Bernard's ending of the *Salve* (when taken with the musical setting) to be the 'highest achievement of human art'. And one recalls how scornful Huysmans was in *Là-bas* of the renderings of the liturgy as heard in Paris. Nevertheless, it remains true that it was not what one would have expected from an austere Cistercian.

Citeaux more appropriately restored manual labour, though eventually this was for the most part taken over by lay brothers, the other monks restricting themselves to the choir and the copying of books. Abbot Butler sums up this phase of Benedictine history by writing: 'From the middle of the tenth century until its supremacy was challenged by the Cistercians early in the twelfth, Cluny reigned supreme in the Benedictine world; and for a long time afterward, until modern times, in Black Monk circles the Cluniac presentation of Benedictine life was in its essential lines the accepted theory on which the life of the monasteries was fashioned.' Oderic Vital, who lived during the first half of the twelfth century, estimates that amalgamated with Cluny there were about two thousand monasteries, and though Schmitz thinks this figure an exaggeration, he grants that there were 1,450 of which 1,300 were in France, with the rest scattered through seven or eight other countries. It was, while it lasted, a tremendously powerful aggregation.

A word will be said in a moment about further Cistercian development. It might be pointed out at once that present-day tendencies, while resulting in various congregations – of which we have four in the United States and two in England – are careful to guard against centralization and to insist upon the preservation of autonomy. But of course there is now no need whatsoever for the kind of protection provided by the Cluniac and Cistercian movements of the Middle Ages. Left to themselves it is quite clear that monks can fulfil their functions so as to avoid all grounds for criticism. But lest it seem that some remarks made here indicate that things were not always in the best of conditions among the monasteries, I note that Abbot Butler writes: 'My knowledge of monastic history leads me to the belief that at all times there has been a background of old-fashioned houses in which a very respectable religious life, with good, if not showy observance and real spiritual religion, was being lived in a

quiet way outside the reform circle of the hour.' It is all
too easy to paint in colours that are much too dark. Many
houses completely escaped external interference and the
disruption it caused, or suffered it only briefly, soon
getting back to normal conditions, even when the memory of the wounds inflicted left the monks without that
sense of security so conducive to order and discipline.

Cluny and Citeaux must be said to have taken up centralization mainly to obtain protection for themselves, at
whatever price, though it must be added that there have
been among Benedictines men of the cast of mind that
look upon this as efficient, and efficiency as being always
a good thing. It was so with a scheme introduced in Italy
in the fifteenth century. The plan, as devised by a Venetian, who may have had the Venetian Council of Ten in
mind, was that of forming a congregation and having it
governed by a general chapter, which would meet every
year and be elected for a set term of years. The president
of the council, all the visitators, all the abbots and the
chief officials, such as the priors and the cellarers, were
appointed, not by their abbots but by the general chapter,
and held office for only one year, being no more than
deputies of the chapter to which they all had to render a
strict account. Similarly the monks were not professed
for a particular house but for the congregation, as is the
case with the religious Orders conducted on other than
Benedictine lines. As Butler points out: 'It is evident that
such a system cuts at the root of "commendam"; but it
also cuts at the roots of the traditional Benedictine
family ideal, for this perhaps more thoroughly than ever
before deprived the abbeys of all individual life.'

Most of these offshoots of Benedictinism have died or
declined, and some of them have never been very numer-

ous. Now we see the Black Benedictines in virtually un-
challenged possession of the field as exponents of the
Benedictine idea, though again it must be conceded that
there is no perfect uniformity here, nor is such uniformity
sought. However, one branch of the Benedictines has
shown an exceedingly vigorous life, and in recent years in
the last place where one would look for this to be true:
the United States. The Trappists, or to give them the official title they prefer – probably because they do not greatly
relish being reminded of Rancé and his abbey – the Cistercians of the Strict Observance, have made an astonishing
appeal to Americans. Possibly they are no more austere
than were the monks of Monte Cassino in the sixth century, though that is austere enough, and one might suppose
austere to such a degree as to be a deterrent. However,
that is only incidental: the main thing is that they strive
to make exalted contemplation the primary end of monasticism, combining this with toil of a most laborious kind.
To a considerable extent they have found in Thomas Merton (Father Mary Louis, to give him the religious name
that does not appear on the title pages of his many books)
one capable of giving them immense publicity and therefore of drawing many men to the Trappists. Yet that is an
accident to which too much should not be attached; what
is rather surprising is that his superiors have been shrewd
enough to take advantage of the lucky circumstance.
Nevertheless, when the most is said of such publicity, the
main fact to consider is that none of this would have
availed at all if there did not exist in the American heart
a longing for the deepest founts of spirituality. Though we
should have known our fellow countrymen better than to
have been so thrown off our guard by the discovery, the
discovery may have almost incalculable reverberations.

G

One is, I say, surprised by this discovery, for though the Trappist mode of life has no very great hardships, there are things about it which suggest that it might be hardly likely to appeal to many. Even Thomas Merton, in his recently published diary (published only in excerpts), shows that he often hankers after the Carthusians. The abstinence from meat may involve no special austerity, for plenty of people in the world are vegetarians from choice. Nor need field work do so, and for the same reason. What would seem to be the most difficult feature of the matter is that the monks work together, yet can communicate only by signs (speech being allowed only very rarely, and then merely to an individual) and yet that they even sleep in an open dormitory, or one merely divided into cubicles. The combination of lack of privacy and absolute silence would seem to be past endurance. For though the continuous communality and the other matters mentioned were known at Monte Cassino, it is clear that silence was not so rigorously insisted upon. Though a Black Benedictine abbot could express his private opinion to me that the Trappists are the only Benedictines who really observe the Holy Rule, the opinion generally held by the main body of Benedictines is that the Trappists are not Benedictines at all. It is not for me to decide in such matters, though what I believe may be deduced from other parts of this book.

I do not have positive information on the point, but I imagine that the Trappists of our time have quietly dropped a practice that gave rise to bitter controversy in Rancé's day. It is that which has been called 'fictitious humiliations', something which, to do him justice, was not unknown before he introduced it but which he revived and brought into prominence. Here the Thundering Abbot went back to a quotation from the Scriptures found in the chapter 'On Humility'; 'Thou has proved us, O God, thou hast tried us as silver is tried by fire; thou hast led us into the snare, and hast laid tribulations on our backs.' Of course all spiritual people may expect to be 'tried as by fire', but Rancé laid his stress upon the 'thou hast led us into the snare', deducing that his monks, in order to test their humility, should be accused of some fault of which they were innocent. Dom Mège in his commentary on the Rule, published in 1687, severely condemned this procedure, saying that it was not permissible to use such violent and artificial tests. Indeed the method would seem to be very unfair, and even contrary to the spirit of good will that should prevail in a family. It might also be argued that false accusations, made with however fair an intention, contravene the commandment against giving false testimony against a neighbour. Finally these fictitious humiliations are not what one would expect even of a gentleman, let alone a Christian.

It was so with all secret informing against a brother. In a very serious matter, when the truth is well founded, it might be the duty of one monk to tell his abbot about another, but for 'testing' a man, ordinary observation should amply suffice. The disposition of a novice in any community is carefully scrutinized before he is admitted to vows, but charges that have no basis in fact should never be brought. Rather there should be mutual charity and helpfulness among the brethren, and probably that was generally true even at La Trappe when Rancé was its abbot. It is more than likely that the method of fictitious humiliations was very seldom used and that far too much has been made of it.

In any event this particular practice should be looked

upon as a seventeenth-century aberration and was due to
the laxity that Rancé found (or imagined he found) in
some monasteries. Probably the fact that Rancé had been
one of the common herd of fashionable *abbés* before his
conversion led him afterward into excessive zeal. Nor
perhaps can one quite leave out of account that the mode
of spirituality expounded by St Francis de Sales seemed
to incline some of those who read him without sufficient
attention to the notion that, as the old Protestant hymn
puts it, he was trying to carry people to the skies 'on
flowery beds of ease'. Francis was attempting nothing of
the kind, as anyone will discover who seriously tries to
carry out his teaching; but a fiery, impetuous mind, such
as Rancé's, not unnaturally preferred stricter methods.
And, after all, the reform he initiated has endured with
very valuable results. The Cistercians of the Strict
Observance provide what meets the deep spiritual hunger
of many souls – souls who would not be satisfied with
the moderation and mildness that one associates with the
Black Benedictines, but which is more commonly and at
least as beautifully a way to God.

Thirteen

The Benedictine Scholar

It should be said at once that scholarship had no part in St Benedict's programme, as it did in that of his contemporary, Cassiodorus, who sought to combine learning with contemplation. While it is true that the Holy Rule enjoins a good deal of reading – perhaps as much as four or five hours a day – this was almost entirely of pious books, though no doubt some general reading went with it, as we can infer from Benedict's own frequent citations of, or allusions to, classical authors. But even if this reading turns out to be a good deal wider than many people suppose, this does not mean that Benedict was greatly interested in scholarship as such. If he shows himself a man not only wise but quietly humorous, this was native to him; as for his capacity for turning a phrase neatly, after all the Scriptures are great literature, among other things, and the Fathers he read – particularly Augustine and Jerome – often put things with great dexterity and pungency. He could have learned from them to do the same, even if that, too, had not been natural to him. But as Benedict's university education at Rome was cut short soon after it began, it would be only reasonable to suppose that what he subsequently acquired should be described as self-education.

It was otherwise with some later founders of religious

institutes. St Ignatius saw so clearly that the work he proposed doing had to have a basis of learning, that we find him as a mature man setting himself to study Latin with schoolboys, and then going to the University of Paris. All the members of the group who took vows with him in the little church on Montmartre on the feast of the Assumption, 1534, were also graduates of that university; this was the type of man he set out from the outset to recruit. Though they had no idea at the time that the work of the Society was to be largely that of conducting colleges, this soon appeared as a work they could hardly avoid. Similarly St Dominic, though he was not particularly deeply versed in anything except theology, gathered followers a good deal above the intellectual average of priests of his day, for only so could the Order of Preachers effectively combat heresy. And if his friend St Francis of Assisi sometimes spoke as though he were against the acquisition of learning by his friars – actually he was only against the possession of too many books as contrary to poverty, and to the kind of learning that might make a man proud – the Franciscans soon emulated the Dominicans. Even in the time of St Francis his Order produced in Bonaventure and Anthony of Padua, scholars who were to receive the title of Doctor of the Church.

This is not to suggest that the Benedictines, even during the early days of Subiaco and Monte Cassino, were an ignorant set of men, for it has already been indicated that those who joined St Benedict were, for the most part, drawn from the higher social ranks. But as they had as yet no apostolic work to perform, they were not called upon to equip themselves for it. However, as Abbot Butler remarks: 'There is no doubt that the steady devotional reading of the Fathers, day in and day out, will in the case of men of ordinary intelligence produce, if not scholarship, a type of culture that may be called intellectual and even learned, in a very real sense.' It may even be that this type of culture is broader than the specialization forced upon some of the other Orders; at the same time it is to be regarded as no more than a by-product of the Benedictine life.

Yet as the Rule makes abundantly clear, such reading was not thought of as Benedictine 'work', for while both are prescribed they are differentiated from one another. Regarding this point Abbot Butler writes: 'That a monk should spend many hours a day reading biographies, even the Lives of the Saints, or history, even Church history, or the Fathers, or the Bible and the commentaries thereon,' will not be considered 'work' in the Benedictine sense. If it comes to that, the writing of occasional articles in magazines, or literary essays or verse, is not held to be work, though it may be 'a very suitable form of recreation for a monk in his hours of repose.' Butler concludes, therefore: 'To be Benedictine work worthy of the name, it must be laborious, patient, thorough, and scholarship in the best sense.' Judged by that standard, the Benedictines have produced many scholars – and Abbot Butler himself was not among the least of them. Nevertheless, the Benedictines do not aim at being a learned Order.

What they have done, however, was to make scholarship possible. More to them than to any other group of men who have ever existed do we owe the preservation of ancient manuscripts. The first efforts of the *scriptorium* were naturally directed toward providing the altar and the choir with the service books they needed, and the library with transcripts of the Fathers and the Lives of the Saints. But the time came when a sufficiency of these had been produced and attention could be given to the copying of the ancient poets, philosophers, and historians. It cannot be claimed that Benedictine monks had much to do with the preservation of Greek manuscripts, for though St Theodore of Canterbury introduced Greek studies into England soon after the conversion of that country, Greek afterward became virtually an unknown tongue in western Europe until after the fall of Constantinople in 1453, and by then Greek texts could be printed. But the Benedictine *scriptorium* was the main instrument in preserving the Latin classics, together with later works in Latin and the vernacular. Were it not for this we would now have a very vague and disjointed idea of our own origins.

Other religious orders of the Middle Ages helped in this work but only in a subsidiary way, and they came into the field only after the Benedictines had already saved the chief manuscripts from oblivion. The Dominicans and Franciscans had too many external occupations to be able to spare much time for the copying of books; therefore most of what they needed was secured from Benedictine sources. And immediately before the Jesuits appeared upon the scene printed books made the *scriptorium* out of date. Yet it should be remembered that for a considerable time the printer himself had nothing to put upon his presses except what he obtained from the monks. As for the great libraries of the world, their invaluable manuscript collections come almost wholly from the monasteries. These would have been still more abundant – at any rate so far as England was concerned – had it not been for the wanton destruction that accompanied the expropriation under Henry VIII. Thomas Cromwell was enough of a connoisseur of beautiful things to appreciate a richly illuminated Book of Hours, which, moreover, he recognized to be valuable, but the ordinary service books were sold for a few pence, as we might sell old newspapers as of no further use. Therefore shopkeepers used them to wrap up their wares; we may be sure that many a monkish chronicle was similarly scrapped as so much junk. For this reason alone Abbot McCann is able to say: 'For the early Middle Ages, the period of their greatest influence, the Benedictine monasteries were the chief cultural centres of Europe.'

This, however, is by no means all. We know that the Council of Aachen, held in 817, provided for two kinds of monastic schools: those for boys who intended to enter the monastic state, and for those who did not. The usage varied from country to country and from century to century, but this was the general scheme for a long while, until, in fact, the chantry priests were also able to help in the educational effort. In England, for example, we find that the abbeys of Reading, Bury St Edmund, and St Albans maintained schools described as 'for the poor' – presumably not exactly that, but schools which made very light charges – while Glastonbury, Hyde, and Winchester, served as schools for the sons of the nobility. Indeed, the Benedictine schools formed the germ of what were to become the universities of Oxford and Cambridge, and much the same is true of the origin of nearly all, if not all without qualification, of the universities of Europe. We know, too, that when the universities came into being they were largely staffed by Benedictines and that a high proportion of their students were young monks. Schmitz in the fifth volume of his *Histoire* gives some interesting figures on this, saying that from 1449 to 1538 Oxford University had as students 213 Benedictines, 67 Franciscans, 53 Dominicans, 52 Cistercians (who were also, of course, Benedictines), 32 Augustinians, and 12

Carmelites. The Benedictine contribution to the intellectual life of Europe has been quite incalculable.

Abbot Butler has been quoted as affirming that from the time of their foundation Benedictines must have derived, if not precisely learning or scholarship from the reading enjoined by the Rule, at least a broad general culture. But he says elsewhere: 'It has to be recognized that ... Benedictine scholars have been at all times singular — one here, one there; the idea of a universally learned Benedictine body is a myth, due to its partial, though very brilliant realization among the Maurists of the seventeenth and eighteenth centuries.' Here he is obviously reluctant to claim too much, with the result that he does not really claim enough. It is true, of course, that, in the nature of things, no entire group of men will have the special aptitudes called for by profound and exact scholarship, but only a few among them. A better way of putting it might be to say that a steady glow was sought rather than the coruscation which, even under the most fortunate conditions, was not to be encountered very often. If it comes to that, the vast majority of men and women who today succeed in obtaining the Ph.D. degree merely acquire the technique of scholarship but have no assurance that they will be able to put it to any very important use. Most of them produce nothing after they have painfully ground out a dissertation. And of those who conscientiously (or of necessity) continue to produce, their work is commonly so dull that it would be preferable if they held their peace. Such scholars as the Benedictines produced were fortunately of a very different stamp.

Perhaps the most charming of them all was one of the earliest, St Bede, whom the world has chosen to call the 'Venerable Bede', not because he lived to any advanced age, for he died when he was only sixty-two, but rather because of the special veneration in which he was held. He tells us himself that he entered the abbey at Jarrow when he was seven, being donated by his father, that he was ordained deacon when he was nineteen and priest when he was thirty-five. He seems never to have held any office, and one imagines that his fellow monks recognized that he should be free to follow his own bent. This gave him in the end not only canonization but the honour of being the only Englishman to receive the title of Doctor of the Church.

That honour he obtained perhaps mainly for his scripture commentaries. Yet his chief literary production was his *Ecclesiastical History of the English Nation*. For much of the period covered in this work Bede is almost our only authority and certainly our most reliable authority. His perfect honesty is evident on every page, though of course that is not enough for a historian, as with the best of good faith he may be inaccurate or gullible or have personal crotchets. What might be called the last occasionally do appear, as when he speaks with some asperity of the Celtic missionaries. We have to conclude that he was justified in his complaints, for he was obviously a man of the sweetest good temper. Moreover, he shows throughout his book a remarkable sense of historical method, though he had nobody to instruct him in this. He not only cites such authors (the British monk, Gildas, for instance) upon whom he can draw, but tells us, when there were no written records, as was usually the case, just who his informants had been. Finally, he had his manuscript carefully gone over by those most capable of detecting any inadvertent errors it might contain. One can see that he spared no pains at arriving at the exact truth. The result is not a dry, factual chronicle, but one of the most fascinating works of its kind ever produced, a work of art in which Bede unconsciously displays his own beautiful character.

He also supplied us with what one must suppose is a complete list of his writings. These not only comprise the history and the scriptual commentaries mentioned but some exercises in biography, an *ars poetica* and a number of poems both in Latin and Anglo-Saxon. These last, with a poet's vanity (which in Bede's case is very engaging) he offered to send to anyone who wished to have a copy. What shines out clearly – even if we could not find this in his *Ecclesiastical History* – is that Bede was a man of wide and varied interests and an altogether delightful person. Even regarding his choir duties he had a way with him that is altogether his own, for Alcuin, after a visit to England, wrote to the monks at Jarrow: 'Our master and your patron is reported to have said, "I know that the angels come to the canonical hours and to the assemblies of the brethren. What if they did not find me among my brothers? Would they not have reason to say, *Ubi est Baeda?* Where is Bede? Why does he not come with the brethren to the appointed services?" ' His life has been told in a single sentence: *Semper legit, semper scripsit, semper docuit, semper oravit* – he was always reading, always writing, always teaching, always praying.

The account of his death given by his disciple Cuthbert shows that he was to the end the very same man he had been in health. He fell seriously ill two weeks before Easter, but in spite of this did not cease his daily lectures, passing the rest of the day (and most of the night as well) in singing psalms. 'I solemnly protest,' wrote Cuthbert, 'never have I seen or heard of anyone who was so diligent in thanksgiving.' This went on until the Tuesday before

Ascension Thursday. Then, realizing that he was now sinking, Bede tried to hurry the young monk who was taking down at his dictation the translation of the Gospel of St John, the work that was in hand. Yet evidently he was forced to stop every now and then, for finally one of those present said, 'Dearest master, one chapter is still missing; can you bear our asking you about it?' The reply came, 'I can bear it; take your pen and be ready to write quickly.' So the day passed until evening, except for Bede's dividing up among the monks a few small gifts. At last the scribe had to tell him that there was still one sentence not written. Again the answer came, 'Write it quickly.' Then with a *consummatum est*, he lay back with his head in the young monk's hands, saying, 'It is very pleasant for me to sit facing my old praying-place and thus to call upon my Father.' So sitting, half reclined on the floor of his cell, he sang the *Gloria*, and with the words 'Holy Ghost' on his lips he quietly died. He was a scholar monk intent upon his task until his last breath.

Abbot Gasquet who, before he was created a cardinal, was appointed head of the Papal Commission for the Revision of the Vulgate, and as such has special authority to speak, points out that from Bede and his fellow monks of Wearmouth and Jarrow comes the best and most accurate manuscript of the Vulgate, the *Codex Amiatinus*. He shows just why this was 'a scientific achievement of the highest quality', for it involved a critical sifting of all the versions available, so as to obtain the most accurate text. 'This,' says the Cardinal, 'was, indeed, an undertaking proper to tax the highest scientific qualities of any age.' It is astonishing that it came out of a country so recently converted from heathenism; it shows how thorough was the Christianizing of England by St Augus-

tine and his successors. More than that, it shows that
with the introduction of Christianity there also arrived a
rich culture. For the conversion of England was an
entirely Benedictine project, except for what the Celtic
monks in the west and north may have contributed.

Though Bede was the greatest of these English Benedictine scholars, it is evident that there were others, some
of whom were a good deal earlier than Bede. For instance,
at the Bodleian may be seen the earliest manuscript book
produced in England. It is a copy of the Holy Rule
written at Canterbury about 700. The best extant copy,
however, is the one made at Aachen about a hundred
years later. Though Abbot Butler says that notable
scholars appeared among his fellow monks only now and
then, the Maurists, of whom mention has already been
made, operated as a group. As such they cannot be left
out of our relation, even if space obliges the omission
of many illustrious names.

It must not be imagined, however, that even this celebrated French congregation of abbeys produced nothing
but *savants*. In their case, as in that of all Benedictine
abbeys, a man entered primarily with the purpose of serving God in the monastic state. Only a relatively small
proportion of the Maurists became learned to any extraordinary degree, for t would be impossible to expect
more. But even after this admission has been made, the
total number was astonishingly large. Butler's own article
in the *Encyclopædia Britannica* lists two hundred and
twenty writers and more than seven hundred works – all
of the scholarly sort that can only be the fruit of many
years of toil. Nor does this take into account the many
anonymous collaborators – who were undoubtedly a
good deal more numerous than those whose names appear

on a title page – or even the works begun by others which the Maurists brought to completion. As an instance of this category is the great Latin dictionary or *Glossarium* of Charles du Fresne du Cagne (1610–88), for the Benedictines added seven others to the three volumes he left. Even so, the *Glossarium* must be considered merely as a minor offering when compared with some of the others to be mentioned.

It must be remembered that though the Maurist congregation comprised one hundred and eighty monasteries, most of them were small – probably at no time did the whole group have more than a couple of thousand members – and that during the whole period of their existence there were hardly more than eight thousand Maurists. Though one may say that of the two hundred and twenty writers, perhaps no more than fifty are to be reckoned as outstanding, still the atmosphere of the congregation was scholarly, for many who personally wrote nothing performed the laborious spadework for those who did. In general we may say that this Benedictine achievement, like the rest of the enterprises upon which they embarked, was anonymous.

Much of its success was due to the backing the Maurists obtained from Cardinal Richelieu and to some extent from Cardinal de la Rochefoucauld. Richelieu found in Abbot Tarrisse, the superior general of the congregation from 1630 to 1648, the very man to carry out his ideas, which of course were those of Tarrisse himself. Abbot Butler explains what was in the mind of this learned monk: 'Surprise is often expressed at the number of exceptionally able men who all at once, about the year 1660, appeared in the ranks of the Maurists, so as to enable them to undertake and to carry out so many vast works of erudition and permanent value. The reason is not far to seek. Thirty years before, in the days of Dom Gregory Tarrisse, the Maurist superiors had determined that their congregation should, for the service of the Church, undertake several great works, chiefly critical and historical, especially new editions of the Fathers and a history of the Order. For thirty years the work of preparation had been silently going on, young monks of promise being specially trained in habits of research and of organized work, and the foundations being laid deep and solid. As yet little had been produced, for they aimed at forming not authors but a school.' In short, we have here a notable graduate school, one conferring no degrees and in which personal applause was not sought, but perhaps being all the better for that.

The Maurist Abbey of Saint-Germain-des-Prés became the intellectual centre of France, one might almost say of Europe. There every Sunday afternoon would gather scholars of almost every shade of opinion for the exchange of views – Port Royalists and Ultramontanes and Gallicans and sceptics, all so to speak on neutral territory. And learned men from other Orders – Jesuits and Dominicans and Franciscans – and with them not a few laymen, would drop in to take part in the delightful discussions, for such an opportunity was not to be found elsewhere and so none could afford to miss it. We may see in these informal gatherings after Vespers the creation of the modern school of historical criticism. Nor does the querulous complaint that the abbey was more like a literary club than a religious house have any real validity, for these assemblies were only on Sunday afternoons, though a scholar passing through Paris might arrive at almost any time at Saint-Germain-des-Prés to consult one of the monks about a particular problem. The monastic life was regular; research did not interfere with the choral

Office but had become for these monks the equivalent of the *scriptorium* of ancient days.

Butler tells us that what was actually published was only a portion of what was planned or in course of preparation. The Maurists' main achievement was undoubtedly a new edition of the Fathers. And though Migne has superseded this, Migne could not have done his work had not the Maurists preceded him. At any rate Migne's Greek and Latin patrology is more complete than any other, though it has its defects, and is in some instances below the critical standard that the Maurists maintained. In the Bibliothèque Nationale at Paris there are hundreds of manuscript volumes of materials gathered by these monks, and in these the learned societies of France are still quarrying. For the histories of the French provinces there are eight hundred volumes; two hundred and thirty-six for a *Trésor Genéalogique*; thirty-one for a history of the Crusades; ninety on Benedictine antiquities; and materials for eight folio volumes of *Concilia Galliae*, only one of which had been printed by 1789. 'Nor,' says Butler, 'was this all. In the last years, at the request of the civil power, the Maurists undertook the vast scheme of a *Trésor des Chartes*, or copies of every important ancient document in France.'

We find here a stupendous corporate effort of a unique kind, to which most lamentably the outbreak of the French Revolution put an abrupt end. No religious institute had ever previously attempted anything like it, nor is it likely to be attempted again, for it is scarcely conceivable in the modern world that so large a group could be spared from other pressing activities. Henceforth it seemed the monastic scholar must be prepared to work in isolation, or at best with one or two collaborators, be he a Benedictine or a Jesuit. However, it would be rash to make any prophecy, for who could have foretold that a raw young man from the Abruzzi named Baronius would have been assigned, while still a layman, to lecture at St Philip Neri's Oratory on the history of the Church, and that Philip, that most whimsical of souls, would have perceived that this young man, after his ordination, would produce the twelve monumental volumes of his *Annales*. For Baronius this led to a cardinalate, which he would have liked to have been free to refuse, and it even brought him within an inch of being elected pope. He only just managed to save himself by clinging to the pillars of the consistory; otherwise he would have been made pope by acclamation. But we are much more likely to see another Baronius (very rare though men of his type are) than another group such as the Maurists.

What we have seen, especially in Europe, is a number of recent Benedictine scholars of another sort, and for these we should be duly grateful. These men are at their best with the relatively small single volume, which they contrive to write with grace and charm. From some of them quotation has been made in these pages. Yet it must be added that though Downside Abbey alone has had in succession as abbot, Gasquet, Butler, and Chapman, each has worked as an individual, often disagreeing with one another on this or that minor point, and being able to express that disagreement in such a way that a fresh flower has been added to friendship. The most one can say (if we also remember McCann, the titular abbot of Westminster) is that there is a 'school' of English Benedictine authors. Even if they attempted a corporate enterprise, they do not begin to be numerous enough to produce anything on the scale of the Maurists. Even if we add to these the French monks of Farnborough and Quarr Abbeys and the Germans of Buckfast, we still have nothing comparable to the hundred and eighty Maurist houses, and the circumstances of the lives of these modern monks forbid more than the occasional production of a book by a solitary scholar. There is no use complaining, if one wished to complain; rather, we should recognize that, in view of the needs of the modern world, this is probably for the best.

Fourteen

The Blessing of Benedict

THERE IS no doubt that Benedict did bring an incalculable blessing to the world. Just as Monte Cassino has been three times destroyed – most recently by American bombs in the course of the last war – so Benedictinism shows a perennial power. Well might Monte Cassino's motto be *Succisa virescit*, as it might also be that of Benedictine monks taken as a whole. The oldest form of monasticism that has survived in the West has suffered many vicissitudes, but even today, in the face of many new manifestations of the religious life – each of them valuable, and usually devoted to some special activity – the monasticism of the Holy Rule has amply proved that it is very far from being outmoded, and may well be coming into a period more glorious than any that it has hitherto known. The monk accomplishes his purpose, not by setting any particular object before himself, but simply by trying to reach personal perfection in the quiet old way of the cloister.

We have seen that Benedictine history has been a series of ups and downs. By the twelfth century perhaps the height had been reached, and though the decline that set in soon afterward was so gradual as to escape notice at first – and was even marked in many places by an increase in external grandeur – the grandeur itself contributed to

the undoing of medieval monasticism. Many monasteries
were so prosperous as not to demand much work from
their monks. Moreover, as Schmitz puts it in the third
volume of his *Histoire*: 'The abbey had become a fief and
the abbacy a benefice. . . . Many of the abbeys opened
their doors only to the nobility.' Though they were not
as a rule nearly as wealthy as was imagined, a few of them
were too wealthy for their own good. The monks were
sometimes inclined to be a bit slack, and their holdings
offered a temptation to the powerful personages of the
world who, whether they made merely the partial expropriation of the *in commendam* system in France and Scotland or the absolute confiscation suffered under Henry
VIII in England caused the monks to experience either
some degree of demoralization (or at least disorganiza-
tion) or total suppression.

This is not to say that the monasteries were hotbeds of
iniquity, though naturally it suited Henry VIII's book to
make such charges, in order to give some colour of justification to his own barefaced brigandage. But no doubt
delinquencies of one sort or another could be discovered,
for the monks were human beings with some tendency to
human shortcomings. The faults reproved were of greatly
varying kinds, a few being really reprehensible, but most
indicating no more than negligence. This is now pretty
generally established, though a Coulton will always be
able to heap on one platter such scandals as he can discover. In any event, this sort of accusation should be esti-
mated in the same way as we read the newspapers: the
report of a few crimes merely means that they provide
news, whereas the virtue of a hundred thousand ordinary
people passes without comment. Three or four words
might be the whole of the report issued by Cromwell's

prying visitors when the religious were faithful to their rule, whereas many pages would be given to the cases of monks (only a very small proportion of the community) who were not to be commended. However, at the time of the Reformation, when the monasteries were handled most roughly, they had largely regained their old standing. Schmitz says, 'With the fourteenth century we reach the most sombre period of Benedictine history.'

Some of the English monks who were uprooted during the sixteenth century managed to enter communities in Spain or Italy or the Low Countries. Most of the others, not very heroic men, found it convenient to accept the new religious arrangements, though probably most of these hoped and believed, as did many people, that the storm would eventually blow itself out. To them it was hardly conceivable that they had lost forever what they and their country had always known. Nevertheless, monasticism had been struck a heavy though not a fatal blow: in Spain and Italy and parts of Germany things went on as formerly, and in France there shone the glory of the Maurists. It was the French Revolution, coming more than two hundred and fifty years later, that seemed to give monasticism its death blow. Then most monks accepted the Civil Constitution of the Clergy, under which they could function only as parish priests; also all such priests were *ipso facto* excommunicated. Thirty Maurists, with their superior general, were among those massacred at the Carmes prison, and were beatified as martyrs; ten other Benedictines of Paris were guillotined; and at least twenty-four others are known to have perished in the provinces.

Nor was the lot of the Benedictines much better during the Napoleonic régime, though Napoleon did not resort to capital punishment. Wherever the Emperor extended his conquests he ejected the monks, with the exception of a few who, he decided, might be useful for work in the hospitals. To condense the dolorous story, at the opening of the nineteenth century of the thousands of Benedictine monasteries that had existed only thirty remained. Well might a man have thought that when their members (amiable old gentlemen, no doubt, but quite anachronistic in the modern world) had died out, monasticism would be extinct. It was even confidently expected by many people that the pope of the time would be the last the world would ever see.

It soon became evident, however, that monasticism, though cut down, was going to rise again. And it was eminently fitting that the process should begin in England, the first country to be converted by Benedictine missionaries. Yet this was by way of an accident: French *émigrés* from the Revolution found a shelter there, and it was for this reason that Ampleforth was established in 1802 and Downside thirteen years later. England benefited again when, because of a new expulsion of religious orders from France early in the twentieth century, new English abbeys were founded, for instance Belmont in England itself and Fort Augustus in Scotland. Now there is what amounts to a galaxy of English abbeys – Belmont and Ramsgate and Ealing Priory among them – in addition to which there are two, Quarr and Farnborough, that are French in origin, and another, Buckfast, whose monks are for the most part German. To complete the picture, or rather the sketchy account given here, an Anglican Benedictine community on Caldey Island came into the Catholic Church in a body and is now settled at Prinknash Abbey near Gloucester. It must be remembered that there are

also several abbeys of Benedictine nuns. English Benedictine life is decidedly flourishing again, after its long
exile on the Continent.

In France the new turn of affairs came when Abbot
Guéranger established the abbey of Solesmes in 1833.
And in the Catholic parts of Germany the Wolter brothers
began the work of reconstruction at Beuron in 1863,
when ex-King Louis I urged the return of monks to
Bavaria. The king did even more, for the missionary
society founded under his name as the *Ludwig-Missions-
verein* was not only extremely generous to the general
work of the Church in the United States but was the chief
backer of Boniface Wimmer when, in 1846, he started
near Pittsburgh what is now known as the Archabbey of
St Vincent, from which centre have radiated all the other
houses of the American Cassinese Congregation. At the
outset they addressed themselves mainly to the Germans
of the locality, looking not only after their spiritual but
their material needs. But now the American Cassinese
Congregation (which has no connection with Monte
Cassino but has taken its name merely in a complimentary
way) has extended its charity by coming to the aid of the
often hard-beset American Catholics of the Eastern Rite
by adopting that rite in one of its dependent priories; and
recently the Congregation of St Otilia for Foreign Missions
has been established in Newton, New Jersey. Another
Benedictine Congregation, the Swiss-American, has also
flourished, its main centre at St Meinrad, Indiana, and
this abbey has recently been made into an archabbey.
Connected with most of these abbeys, whatever the congregation may be, one will usually find a college, if not
in actual being then at least projected; and in several
instances the monks conduct the diocesan seminary.

The inception of the work of Wimmer in America came about in rather a strange way, or was at least proposed by a somewhat eccentric personage. This was Peter Henry Lemcke, who had been an assistant to Prince Gallitzin, a Russian priest who preferred to be known as Mr Smith. While on a visit to Europe in 1845 Lemcke met Wimmer and promised to give him a large tract of land for the building of a monastery, and also to become a Benedictine himself. Both promises were carried out, yet there could hardly have been a less stable Benedictine than Lemcke. However, his wanderings here, there, and everywhere must be admitted to have resulted in the establishment of other monasteries, though after the sixties we find him the pastor of St Michael's and then of St Henry's Church, Elizabeth, New Jersey, where Orestes Brownson and his family were among his parishioners. At the age of eighty he retired to his old haunts in the Alleghenies, where he began to serialize an autobiography which, on account of its excessive frankness, was discontinued after a few issues. He gave the remainder of the manuscript to a friend, but apparently it has been lost. He died in his eighty-seventh year, in 1882.

One of the notable features of American Benedictinism is the great impetus it has given to what is called the Liturgical Movement, to restore the liturgy to its proper place in Catholic life. This has met with marked success in the Middle West, where the Benedictines have their main centres. If to a great extent this has occurred in districts where the Germans congregated – the main reason that German monks settled among them in the first place – this is also partly because German Catholics retained far better than the Irish of the Eastern cities an appreciation of what the liturgy means. It is probably a good deal more because they were so largely under the tutelage of Benedictines, who held to the principle of the Holy Rule that nothing is to be preferred to the *Opus Dei*. It must not be imagined, however, that the liturgical spirit is either German or peculiarly Benedictine; it is simply Catholic. It represents a restoration of the balance after the 'age of devotions'. In many ways it represents a return to pre-Reformation piety, serene, secure, and solid.

From England has come the foundation of the Priory at Portsmouth, Rhode Island, with its fine preparatory school, with another priory, that of St Anselm's at Washington, coming from the Abbey of Fort Augustus in Scotland. The American Cassinese have also undertaken the evangelization of the Bahamas, where the bishop and all the clergy are Benedictines, with the exception, I understand, of a Franciscan who lives more or less as a hermit. This is true also of the Isle of Pines. Going into Canada, one finds an abbey in Saskatchewan, which is affiliated to the United States group, and the Abbaye de Saint-Benoît du Lac, which belongs to the French congregation. St John's at Collegeville, Minnesota, has dependent priories in Mexico City, Puerto Rico, and Japan.

But this is by no means all: English monks have done the pioneer work in Australia and New Zealand, and in Africa have established missions in the island of Mauritius, Madagascar, and South Africa, while Benedictines from Munich have gone to Tunis, and in East Africa the congregation of St Otilia, after working at Dar-es-Salaam, have transferred themselves to Zululand. Similarly one may find a Swiss abbey in the Cameroons and other Benedictines in Portuguese Angola. Their missionaries were, of course, expelled with all others from China when the Communists gained control. It would take too long to enumerate what has been done by monks in Central and South America, my main object being to give some indication of what has been happening in the English-speaking world. But enough has been said to make it clear that work of this sort did not end in the early Middle Ages, but that, when their services are needed, Benedictines still carry out missionary enterprises.

A reference has been made to the attempt on the part of Leo XIII to reorganize Benedictines along lines which pointed to the creation of a 'general'. It need scarcely be said that the project caused a good deal of consternation among Benedictines, who naturally supposed that the formation of the Pope's confederation of congregations would undermine their cherished principle of autonomy and transform all Benedictine houses into part of an 'Order' in the ordinary sense of the term. So far, however, all fears on this score have been falsified; the Abbot Primate is *ex officio* head of the Roman College of St Anselm's, in which capacity he has plenty to do. Moreover, it has been discovered that the position he holds in Rome, with the prestige it confers, has been useful to Benedictine abbeys all over the world, as the Primate is able to facilitate any business they may have to transact with the Holy See. That the Primate presides over the regular meetings of the abbots does not mean that he has any real jurisdiction over them.

A word should be said about the Benedictine oblates, who are, I believe, canonically classified with the tertiaries of such religious Orders as admit lay men or women or secular priests to an association with them, under which they have some share in the merits of the Order and the right to be buried in its habit. But there is this great difference: St Benedict wrote only one Rule, and though it is obviously impossible for those living in the world with other obligations to observe it in the same way as monks and nuns, they can at least live according to the spirit of that Rule. Each oblate does what he finds to be possible in his particular case; no more is demanded of him than that.

These oblates are not a very numerous body, and indeed the various bodies of tertiaries vary widely in numbers, those of the Franciscans amounting, so I understand, to two or three millions, while the Dominicans and Carmelites have deliberately followed a policy of much more strict selection. All of the tertiaries, however, are alike in this: they have a special rule produced for them at a given date, whereas the oblates came into being by degrees and it would seem almost by accident.

It might further be explained that many tertiaries live a conventual life. Indeed of the many Dominican and Franciscan Sisters the only ones ever seen are tertiaries, those of the Second Order being among the most strictly enclosed of religious. Should one call at their convents, one is able to speak to them only from behind a grille. This absolute seclusion does not prevail among oblates in the few instances they live in a community. Thus in 1384 there was founded by St Frances of Rome the Tor di Specchi, which is (or used to be) a group of very aristocratic ladies who took no vows, but, like the rest of oblates, made their 'oblation', and who had no enclosure. Moreover, though they were affiliated with the Abbey of Santa Maria Nuova in Rome, they had the privilege of being free from the jurisdiction of the abbot. St Frances, their foundress, had been married at twelve and is said never once, during her forty years of married life, to have annoyed her husband – which one is tempted to say is almost enough in itself for canonization. In addition to such a community one often comes across an oblate who lives in a religious house, taking part in its choral recitation of the Office, but yet retaining an oblate's freedom. In his last years the famous novelist Huysmans was a man of this type.

The oblates, though their formal obligations are not onerous, nevertheless have to undergo a full year of novitiate, and when they make their oblation sign the document of their profession upon the altar itself, just as do Benedictine monks and nuns, so that it cannot be lightly regarded. They constitute a real part of the Benedictine community; they promise 'conversion of manners' though this must be understood in less strict a sense than is true of Benedictines who are religious in the full sense, which the oblates are not.

Just how and when they came into being is not easy to say. We cannot assign a date, as we can that of 1221, when St Francis of Assisi drew up a special rule for his tertiaries. But this much seems to be likely: that from the outset all those working for the monastery, even in the status of slaves, were regarded as members of the monastic family. Still more was this true of later times when the institution of slavery withered away, and the monastery was obliged to employ a certain number of servants. These – and the slaves before them – might acquire something of the character of 'familiars'; in any case they were God's children, and were welcomed to share, to the degree that they wished or were capable of, in the services of the monastery. In the course of time the more pious among them were given an affiliation with the abbey; without deliberate design, but in accordance with the nature of the case, the oblates came into being.

From that point an extension of the idea was readily

admissible. Friendly neighbours who stood close to the monks were naturally drawn into their orbit. We see something like this situation even among the seventeenth-century Jesuits in Canada, with their *engagés*, pious laymen who were willing to help the Fathers in the mission fields and who did everything from building and hunting to serving as catechists or an armed guard; and the *donnés*, who were engaged more closely in the work, being almost like lay brothers in that they received no salary, yet were not bound in any way. Somewhat similarly the Carthusians up to 1582 had laymen living in their monasteries, giving themselves completely to the service of the monks, and these men, officially known as *rediti*, were often referred to as 'oblates', though without being so in the Benedictine meaning of the term. I have seen in some of the abbeys of the Swiss-American Congregation youths or boys presumably being educated there with the idea that they might eventually feel inclined to enter the novitiate, with a status, in so far as I could gather, not unlike that of those in a minor seminary. They also were called oblates.

Ordinarily, however, one understands by the term Benedictine oblate what I have described: men or women living in the world as ordinary Christians, but attached to a particular abbey, not, of course, bound by monastic obligations, though promising conversion of manners. Poverty and chastity (in the sense that they apply to all) are, of course, expected of them, but to the degree that their state in life permits. That is, there is no restriction of married life and the poverty looked for can be only poverty of spirit, though in the case of oblates both of these virtues are given further force from the fact that they seek to model their lives, in so far as this is possible, according to the Holy Rule. As to obedience, presumably their abbot could lay specific demands upon them, but I have never heard of his doing so, and indeed this would not seem to be very practicable in their case. Under their spiritual director they meet regularly for conferences, but it is more important that they assist at Mass as frequently as possible, and that they say as much of the Divine Office as is convenient. Some very exemplary oblates who have plenty of time at their disposal say it all, but most oblates can manage no more than the Little Office, of which probably the majority can recite in private no more than Prime as part of their morning prayers and Compline at night. Even this much, and the wearing under their clothes of a small scapular made from the same material as is used for the Benedictine habit, serves to remind oblates of what they are, and so foster a better Christian life than they might otherwise attain. They may be also asked to contribute to this or that good work undertaken by the abbey, but there are no dues of any kind. Their status is so light a burden as hardly to be felt, and the spiritual benefits they obtain are very great. Nothing is fastened upon them under pain of sin except what is obligatory on all Christians.

If the monastic life be considered as one of contemplation, though it usually also has a good deal of activity, that of the oblates is obviously an active life, yet need not exclude a certain amount of contemplation. If it comes to that, even those who are in the quiet of the cloister, and are hedged around with regulations that are conducive to contemplation, rarely arrive at mystical experience. The whole matter deserves more than a huddled mention at the close of this little book. All that it is possible to say here is that those who are provided with all the advantages usually fail to reach the desired goal, and not necessarily for want of strenuous effort, whereas God's greatest graces sometimes come upon those one might suppose are too much occupied with social and other duties to be able even to glance in that direction. Madame Acarie in the seventeenth century ended, it is true, as a Carmelite nun and is now beatified, but she became a mystic of a high order and inspired others during the many years previously when as wife and mother she lived in fashionable circles. It was somewhat so also with Philip Neri, who for nearly sixty years was at anybody's beck and call, day or night, and who yet in spite of all the turmoil – or even those exhibitions of fantastic humour so characteristic of him – maintained what seems to have been an unbroken union with God. In the same way it may be supposed that much the same might be possible to the workman at his bench, the housewife in her kitchen.

Fifteen

Benedictine Spirituality

Dom Philibert Schmitz is able to list in an appendix to the second volume of his *Histoire* about eleven hundred Benedictine monks and nuns who have been canonized or beatified. In his list he does not put down some names that are in the *Oblate Manual* issued by St John's Abbey, Collegeville, Minnesota. In that I find that of Etheldred, the King of Mercia who died in 716, and whose only claim for inclusion is, so far as I know, that he was a benefactor. We have in the same month in which his feast is celebrated that of Blessed Mafalda, Queen of Castille, and for July 15 St Henry, the second emperor of that name. These and other royal saints were presumably oblates, and if really such should have been included, but I can find no scrap of evidence that St Thomas More was an oblate, and the Franciscans claim him as a tertiary (again without definite proof). But without going into such questions, Schmitz's roll contains incomparably more names than any other Order could produce. This, of course, does not mean that those listed, whether as formal religious or affiliates, prove that the Benedictines were holier than other people. Rather, it indicates that for several centuries Benedictines were the only religious, and a religious has at least ten times more chance of being raised to the altars of the Church than has a secular priest, and a hundred times more chance than

H

a lay person – unless, of course, martyrdom is involved.

Moreover, during the early centuries the present careful, not to say cautious, 'process' now called for before beatification or canonization was not demanded. The result was that many good men and women obtained their honour by a popular local cult that has never been officially recognized by the Church, though no objection is raised to what may have been done in the past. St Philip Neri, who died in 1595, was perhaps the last saint to be canonized by acclaim (for it was virtually that in his case), and this was winked at by the Holy See, despite the decrees of Urban VIII on the subject, as it was recognized, as soon as he had died, that his eventual canonization would take place as soon as some other cases already pending had been disposed of. Behind all those in the Martyrology are the 'great cloud of witnesses', 'the host that no man can number', those whose very names are unknown but whom we invoke on All Saints' Day. However, what will be attempted in this chapter is not the exaltation of Benedictine sanctity – for nobody can assess that properly – but merely an assessment of the character of Benedictine spirituality.

Perhaps the first thing to say is that this type of spirituality, which was the norm during the Middle Ages, was almost completely unsystematized. About all one can say of these early saints – and it is a great deal – is that their souls were nourished by the liturgy. It is true that St Augustine, St Gregory the Great, and St Bernard wrote much about the mystical life, but it was only later that a 'method' seemed to manifest itself. In the fourteenth century we come upon at least two Dominican friars who carried the matter further, and even they were surpassed by the Dominican tertiary, St Catherine of Siena, who, while living in her parents' house, had astonishing mystical experiences. But the seventeenth-century Franciscan Joseph of Cupertino even surpassed St Catherine, if mysticism is to be measured by the manifestations that sometimes accompany it: voices and visions and bilocation and the rest, in Joseph's case especially levitation. St Teresa of Avila who, with St John of the Cross, is among the greatest exponents of the mystical method, though she underwent some of the mystical concomitants, resisted them, in so far as this was within her power. As for her near contemporary, St Philip Neri, who was obliged to read a joke book before saying Mass to bring him down to earth, and who even so was often lifted into the air while standing at the altar, and was sometimes seized by an ecstasy if he gave more than a passing look at a picture of Christ, never ceased most emphatically to deprecate the accidental phenomena that may accompany mystical experience as being of no importance, and perhaps as being even a danger. It is to this belief that modern writers on the subject strongly incline.

So it is also with such matters as the stigmata. Though there have been instances where the genuineness of this is not open to question, there is reason to believe such manifestations sometimes may be induced by hysteria, or even be downright fraud. Accordingly the Church treats reported visions with great reserve, being well aware that they may be merely imaginary; indeed, the Church invariably starts with the supposition that they *are* imaginary, until they are conclusively shown to be otherwise. What is worth noting is that most of the early mystics had no experience of this kind to relate. St Thomas Aquinas only once, so far as we know, heard a Voice speaking to him from the altar, and that shortly before he died. Of St

Benedict we know also of only one vision. This was of the kindled sky at night, something more brilliant than the sun, which was followed by his seeing the soul of Abbot Germanus. The *Dialogues* describes this as the whole world being gathered up before the eyes of Benedict in a single ray of light. In reply to the question put by Peter the Deacon Gregory explained: 'All creation is bound to appear small to a soul that sees the Creator. Once it beholds a little of His light, it finds all creatures small indeed.' Gregory does not say that Benedict had had a glimpse of the Beatific Vision, for the sight of that would be unattainable by human beings still on earth, but 'a little of that light'. It was so that St Teresa glimpsed God – as a dazzling point. Yet this was mystical experience of a high order. Abbot Cabrol expresses his regret 'that we have not and shall never have sufficient elements to write the chapter on the spirituality of St Benedict in a satisfactory and complete way; and that this subject remains, like the man himself, in a sort of cloud, in which we discern only the principal features.'

The possibility of occurrences of mystical nature must be admitted; it is also advisable to be cautious about believing in the reality of all we hear of.

There is another aspect of the matter: a vision may be real enough and yet be diabolical. It was so with St Benedict several times, though one gets the impression that, so far from being frightened or even from nervously feeling that he should make 'tests', he took the satanic visitations casually and as incapable of doing any harm. However, one also sees the possibility that at least in some of the cases cited, other explanations may be given. For example in that of the wall that fell upon and killed the young monk building it, this may have happened (as I have said before) because he was an amateur who did not know very much about this sort of work.

I am inclined to think that either St Gregory, or his informants were rather too given to seeing the Devil everywhere. But unlike most people who might feel this way, I think the appalling propensities of the human heart are sufficient to explain most of the evil in the world. Yet the reflection might be made that what might be described as the Gregorian view is more optimistic, in that it takes it for granted that, even if men are readily drawn into evil, they have to be drawn by an external force before they go in that direction; that otherwise they would live innocently.

In the above quotation Abbot Cabrol probably means that we are not given even a hint of the kind of systematization evolved by the writers on mysticism who appeared in the sixteenth century. Moreover, still later writers have attempted to present that systematization in an even more orderly fashion, adopting a textbook tone and manner that, so far from being helpful, sometimes strike one as rather arid and even repulsive. However, the division of the spiritual life into the stages of the purgative, the illuminative, and the unitive is undoubtedly correct, but needs some discretion in its application. We might be misled if we think of one climbing a ladder rung by rung, being finished with the rung below when one mounts to the one just above. The truth, of course, is that even those who have attained union with God still need some purgation in this life. Moreover, that union, like the illumination, is not and cannot be constant but is only intermittent. Were it not so, those who seek perfection would be likely to be discouraged from the outset, for they would be looking for something they would not receive, and then, in their disappointment, think that the whole business of contemplation is an illusion.

Such discouragement is quite unnecessary, for though it is true that the mystical is the highest form of the spiritual life, it is clear that not all the saints – indeed, only a relatively small number of them – may be called mystics. The explanation is a relatively simple one, which I think I can see fairly clearly but which I do not feel competent to expound. This much, however, I may venture to say: as the word is used by some of the textbooks, mysticism is a technique, very valuable to those who can use it, but not indispensable to holiness. While it is certain that the loftier heights of contemplation are reached only by infused grace, Abbot Butler remarks that 'mysticism has a wider meaning; beside the experience of union with God, it may be applied to the whole process of spiritual growth which in special cases issues in this supreme experience. . . . The instinctive belief that such a consummation is possible does influence the lives of many, and induces them to enter on a course of self-discipline and prayer that undoubtedly does spiritualize and ennoble their lives, even though for the most part they do not reach the goal at which they aim. Thus mysticism concerns wider circles than the inmost one of the few who achieve the actual mystical experience.' One gathers that what he says amounts to an affirmation that all good and sincere Christians are constantly handling mysteries. St Paul calls the Sacraments mysteries. Marriage he describes as a 'great mystery'. Christians are constantly on the edge of mystical experiences, even though they may not be consciously aware that this is so. Yet though they could never be called mystics in the strict sense, they may be far advanced on the road to sanctity.

Benedictine spirituality, therefore, is thought of as something within the framework of the Rule. Apart from that it is not systematized and presents no 'method'. Cabrol most appositely quotes from Cassian who was so freely drawn upon by Benedict: 'A monk who often recites the Psalms is so penetrated with the feelings which they express that he no longer seems to be reciting them from memory, but composing them himself, as if they were a prayer drawn from the depths of his heart; or at least it seems that they have been specially written for his case, so that all that happened to David is again accomplished in his own person.' In other words, Benedictine spirituality is liturgical. Even those who came immediately after Benedict, unless we except St Gregory the Great, had little or nothing to say about the 'art' of prayer.

There was no set time for private prayer indicated by the Rule, or even for the meditation now universal in religious houses and the seminaries in which the students during the period of training are expected to model themselves, in so far as this is possible, upon religious. While the Rule, of course, permits and encourages private prayer, it indicates that it should be brief, unless it be prolonged by a special inspiration of grace. No devotional practices, not even devotions to Our Lady, are mentioned, though this does not mean the Benedictine monk did not invoke the Mother of God. Ordinarily, however, it is assumed that the choral Office will suffice – that and spiritual reading. As Schmitz puts it: 'Discretion rules not only the relation of the abbot with his monks, but also their relation with God.' This is not in the least opposed to mysticism, even if one uses the word as some writers insist that it should be used, but it does put the stress elsewhere. St Gregory, an acknowledged master of the mystical life, always used the word contemplation instead, and, though the two words mean much the same thing, the contemplation of the Benedictine is normally attained in the fervent chanting of the choral Office.

This is not to say that the crowd of devotions that have accumulated since the Reformation are not good, for at least all are good that are being used in public church services, though I have come across some merely private devotions that seem unnecessary if not actually silly. But even the devotions that have received episcopal approval are now too many for anybody to attempt them all. Still, there are many excellent people who do their best to say every kind of novena that they come across; there is a very real danger that they may be smothered by them, or at least that their spiritual life may become cluttered up. The reasons for the popularity of these devotions are many, one being that almost every religious institute has a favourite devotion which it seeks to promote; another is that, in Ireland, for instance, during the penal days when Mass could be heard only by stealth, the majority of the faithful could at best say the rosary during the Holy Sacrifice. I would be the very last person in the world to say a word against this (for I say the rosary daily myself), but its recital is not the best way of assisting at Mass. All this created a tradition which has only recently begun to yield ground, no doubt due mainly to the strong recommendations of every Pope since Pius X that the faithful should 'pray the Mass'.

During the Middle Ages a daily attendance at Mass was so common as to come close to being universal, though only very rarely was Holy Communion received. Even in religious communities this was ordinarily but once a week, and often less. But from the frequent references we find to lay people using a 'Book of Hours' it is evident that they said part of the Divine Office, and everywhere the evening service was the saying of Vespers, in which the congregation seems to have taken part. All this was a piety definitely of the Benedictine type; the Middle Ages were what Cardinal Newman called 'the Benedictine centuries'.

About prayer in general St Thomas Aquinas, following St John Damascene, makes what will strike most people as a very surprising statement: that there is only one kind of prayer, petition. They may be right in the sense intended, but the Mass (to go no further) is clearly, in the main, a prayer of thanksgiving even when this is put in petitionary form. Moreover, there is the prayer of supplication, for the forgiveness of sins, and that by which we offer something to God. Ordinarily prayer of petition might have to be put in the lowest category of all, and yet it is the only one most people think of as prayer, often coming to believe, when their prayers seem to go unheard, that it is useless to pray. Yet Our Lord Himself told us to ask our Heavenly Father for our needs, though without having undue solicitude about them. In spite of this – until one comes to the heights of contemplation, concerned wholly with a wordless, imageless adoration – still better is the prayer of praise and thanksgiving; and this is the essence of the liturgy.

St Benedict never used the expression 'the presence of God', but the idea itself often appears in his Rule, as when he tells his monks that they live always under the eye of God. This is perhaps more than the 'Thou the God who hast seen me' of Genesis 16:13, and should be the frame of mind not only of monks but of all Christians. As for the various modes of prayer, the spiritual man will use them all according to circumstances and his needs of the moment; and while using any one of them, he may be suddenly uplifted by some accession of grace, though this is not predictable and still less to be brought about infallibly by the use of some system. The Spirit indeed bloweth as it listeth. St Gregory says that the heights of prayer are much more commonly reached than is supposed, often by altogether untutored people who might be astonished to hear that they are mystics, but who, nevertheless, are what the Trappist Thomas Merton has called 'masked mystics'. The greatest graces are not necessarily the prerogatives of monks or nuns – the majority of whom never attain to them. The most that can be said is that the monastic mode of life, by removing at least some of the usual distractions of the soul, is of all modes of life the one most conducive to contemplation.

One should stress again that contemplation, in the sense of the conscious union of the soul to God, is brief and intermittent. I can think of only one case to the contrary, though there may be others about which I know nothing. St Philip Neri at the end of his long life was given special permission by the Pope to say Mass in a little room that he turned into his private oratory. There at the *Agnus Dei* his server would leave him in darkness, returning after a couple of hours for the completion of the Mass. When the Saint emerged, he was so worn by his experience, whose nature nobody knew, that he looked like an animated corpse, and was obliged to throw himself immediately on his bed for an hour or two.

That is the only case of this kind that we know of, and though Philip derived something from the Benedictines, this last phase of his is very far from the Benedictine tradition of spirituality and asceticism. The Rule discouraged, indeed forbade, any singularity, any mortification (even during Lent) undertaken without the express consent of the abbot. Everything was to be controlled by discretion. Prayer was to be for the most part communal, and asceticism was given an orientation almost exclusively interior, its marks being obedience and still more the humility upon which obedience reposes. Again one must stress the liturgical character of the Benedictine spiritual life. Mr Lindsay ventures to say in the little commentary on the Rule that he prepared for the use of laymen (or oblates): 'Too often, if the layman wishes to do more, and to develop a life of prayer, he tends to seek quantity rather than quality. His prayers, chosen from manuals, become more and more formal and elaborate; he sets time aside for the recitation of rosaries and litanies, adding one special devotion to another until the whole edifice becomes topheavy, and his soul again lies inert under the ruin of its collapse. If his ideas rise beyond vocal prayer, he may attempt meditation, and is once more likely to overburden his spirit with formal schemes built upon preludes and points, colloquies, resolutions, and spiritual bouquets, a severe tax upon his memory, and a cramping influence upon true prayer, the free and open intercourse of the soul with God.' In short, the Benedictine ideal of private prayer, even when some Benedictine spiritual writers have to some extent availed themselves of the systematization that became so much the vogue, is one of simplicity.

Of the writers on spirituality to be treated here – not a great many Benedictines have written about such matters – it might be noted that at least three did not think of themselves as producing books at all. These are St Bernard and the Abbot Marmion of our own day, who

were only addressing their own communities, though no
doubt Marmion may have also had at the back of his
mind from the start that his addresses would afterward be
gathered for publication. The third, Father Baker, certainly had no such idea; it was only long after his death
that someone went through the papers he had left and
arranged and edited them. They were made up of conferences given by him to the English nuns of Cambrai, to
whom he was chaplain. The point is that ordinarily
Benedictines do not write many books of spirituality, for
their own spirituality is a fruit of faithful adherence to the
Holy Rule.

St Gregory the Great, however, still stands as among
the greatest masters of contemplation, in which he fully
exemplifies the Benedictine spirit. In his *Western Mysticism* (not to be confused with his *Benedictine Monachism*)
Abbot Butler offers an excellent analysis of the Saint's
teaching, one that he adumbrates in his earlier book. The
central idea, steadily held to, is that there can be no true
mysticism which is not based upon asceticism, though
this must be understood as interior rather than physical
mortification. Gregory's works have had an enormous
influence upon Catholic religious life if only because he is,
after St Augustine, the Father most frequently drawn
upon in the lessons of the breviary. (St Bernard, judged
by this standard, comes in as a bad third, though he, too,
is utilized in the breviary close on to fifty times.) Whereas
St Augustine provides most of the lessons during the
ferial days of Lent as well, of course, as at other times, it
is St Gregory who is used during the great feasts of
Christmas, Easter, the Ascension, and Pentecost. Priests
and religious cannot help getting saturated with his
thought, even if the majority of them probably never

open one of his works. Schmitz is therefore able to say in the second volume of his *Histoire*: '[Gregory] has been par excellence the director of Christian consciences.'

It must also be remembered that it was St Gregory who as Pope, taking the ancient Gelasian formulary as his base, worked over it, polishing and repolishing, to provide us with the Mass in what is essentially the form as it is now said. This is more and more clearly borne out both by external and internal evidence. When we add to this the work done upon the chant or plain song to which his name is often attached, we see how much we are indebted to him. Again it was a question of revision, but one that resulted in something incomparably better than the chant he revised.

With regard to the breviary, Schmitz tells us in his sixth and concluding volume that this also emanated from the Benedictines at about the end of the eleventh century. This does not mean, of course, that there was no Divine Office until then, for St Benedict gives somewhat detailed instructions in the Holy Rule not only as to how the psalms should be sung but as to their arrangement. And of course in the Desert the monks said the whole of the hundred and fifty psalms of the Psalter every day, whereas Benedict considered it enough for this to be done every week. The breviary was a gathering for the sake of convenience into a single volume of what had hitherto been contained in several: the Psalter, the antiphonary, the responsorial, the hymns and collects, and the lessons and homilies. In doing this the monks made the breviary not only much more easy to use themselves, but gave a great impetus to its general adoption by clerics, though this did not come about as a matter of obigation for some time. The breviary, as we know it, has suffered many revisions, and it is slightly amusing to come upon not only hymns written in sapphics but hymns (produced during the Renaissance) in which heaven, for the sake of an appallingly misguided wish to be 'elegant', is transformed into Olympus, and God the Father Almighty given the soubriquet of Jove. It is true that it happens only very occasionally, but it does happen. Needless to say the Benedictines cannot be charged with even the slightest responsibility in the matter.

St Anselm, born in 1033, was a monk and then abbot of Bec in Normandy and finally, after the Norman Conquest, Archbishop of Canterbury, succeeding Lanfranc, and dying in 1109. He was the third Benedictine Doctor of the Church, those who preceded him being Gregory the Great and Bede. He was eminent as a theologian but also expert in the spiritual life. In his writings we find instead of the slightly cut-and-dried manner that often appeared later in men of his intellectual standing – more particularly after the Reformation had provoked a recoil toward what is termed efficiency – a warmth of feeling that is imparted to the reader. A typical passage from his prayers runs: 'Make me, I beseech Thee, O Lord, to taste by love that which I taste by knowledge; to perceive by affection what I perceive by understanding. Draw me, O Lord, into Thy love, even this whole self of mine. All that I am is Thine by creation, make it to be all thine by love. Behold, O Lord, my heart is before Thee; it striveth, but of itself it cannot do what it would; do Thou all that which of itself it cannot do. Cleave thou unto Him, cleave unto Him earnestly, O my soul! O good Lord, cast her not away. She is sick with hunger for Thy love, do Thou cherish her.'

St Bernard's spirituality, says Butler, was 'simply and solely religious, pure piety, fixed above all on the contemplation of our Lord Jesus Christ as man. Our Lord had been the object of devotion of the older saints and fathers from St Paul downward. . . . But St Bernard dwelt on the sacred Humanity in a way that was all his own, thus opening up the floodgates to the great devotion to Jesus Christ as man that flowed so strongly and characterized so markedly the devotion of the later Middle Ages, and of modern times. . . . Not that such images of Our Lord and of His Cross had ever ceased to be the central object of worship and devotion: but St Bernard was able from the depths of his loving and devout nature, and by his gifts of true inspired poetry and rare eloquence in ardent moving oratory, to impart to it a warmth and colour it had not had before.' This kind of religious sentiment is likely to be regarded with some contempt by such dabblers in mysticism as Aldous Huxley, who seems mainly attracted by the abstract and rarefied concepts of the Orient, but who can find a measure of support from those Christian mystics who, without intending to reject the Bernardian mode, say that supreme mystical moments are devoid of all imagery. It is for this, among other reasons, that the mystic always needs to be on guard, so that what might be described as his private theology is controlled by the dogmatic teaching of the Church.

One may take an example of Bernard's method – there is only space enough for one. And it is characteristically Benedictine in the importance it attached to humility. (That Bernard reversed the order of Benedict's twelve degrees of humility is of no consequence; it is not the order that matters, but the stages he pointed out; and both are derived from Cassian.) This is what St Bernard writes: 'Virginity is a praiseworthy virtue, but humility is more necessary. If the one is counselled, the other is commanded. . . . You can be saved without virginity, but not without humility. The humility, I say, which mourns over the loss of virginity, is pleasing to God; but without humility, I am bold to say, not even the virginity of Mary would have been so. . . . If Mary had not been humble, the Holy Spirit had not rested upon her. It is then evident that she conceived by the Holy Ghost, as she herself declares: *God rewarded the humility of His handmaiden*, rather than her virginity: and I conclude without doubt that it was rather by her humility than by her virginity (where both were pleasing) that she pleased God and was chosen by Him.'

From that quotation one may take a long leap to come to the seventeenth-century Augustine Baker, chaplain of the English nuns at Cambrai. Broadly one might say that Father Baker was Carmelite rather than Benedictine, for one may discern in him a tendency to exalt contemplation to what almost appears at times to be a disparagement of the choral Office. At least he would have something of the air of Carmel did one not know that he had been deeply influenced by the English mystics of the fourteenth century, Richard Rolle and Walter Hilton, as well as by the anonymous author of *The Cloud of Unknowing*, concerning which last Abbot Chapman has written: 'It seems to sum up the doctrines of St John of the Cross two hundred years beforehand.' As I have perhaps made some petulant remarks about Mr Huxley (largely because my admiration for him is frequently overcome by my annoyance with his special brand of intellectual snobbery), I should in justice add that it would be impossible to find a better exposition of *The Cloud of Unknowing* that is in his *Grey Eminence*. Yet despite Father Baker's immediate indebtedness to his English forerunners, he was steeped in John of the Cross and Teresa, and all this led him to turn away to some extent from the Benedictine tradition.

Abbot Butler explains this by saying that at the time Baker wrote he was not unnaturally in reaction against the overelaboration of ceremonies that had set in since the Cluniac heyday, which reaction involved another kind of departure from the Benedictine spirit of simplicity. It was left to Dom Guéranger in the nineteenth century to restore the liturgy to its proper place. Butler's conclusion is: 'Benedictines will be well advised if they take what is positive in both of them: for if we accept all that Fr Baker says of the value and power of internal prayer, and also, as easily we may, all that Dom Guéranger says of the value and power of liturgical prayer, then we shall secure for ourselves a well-balanced Benedictine life of prayer.'

Augustine Baker in his insistence upon a rigorous detachment from all earthly things is closer to St John of the Cross than to St Benedict who was absolutely opposed to any kind of private ownership and laid his stress on this rather than on detachment. I do not say that this detachment is found to the same degree in St John's friend St Teresa, for she always had the keenest possible interest in all the concerns of her brother and his children, and was constantly sending them small presents, of marmalade and the like. Nor can we say that the great St Bernard was very detached when he gave vent to his impassioned grief over the death of his brother Gerard: 'My very bowels are torn away; and it is said to me, "Do not feel any pain." But I do feel pain. . . . I have not the insensibility of a stone, nor is my flesh of bronze. . . . Someone has called this carnal; I do not deny that it is human, just as I do not deny that I am a man. If that does not suffice, then I shall not deny that it is carnal. Nevertheless, I do not at all wish to oppose the decrees of the Holy One. It is not reasonable to declare that I call in question the sentence because I felt the penalty keenly. To feel is human but to repine would be impious.' This moving outburst comes from the man who has been described as the 'last of the Fathers', to which the Abbé Vacandard, the author of one of the best of his biographies, ventures to add that Bernard was as great as the greatest among them. He is certainly not less great because he dared to be so unashamedly a human being. What he said about his brother Gerard calls to mind what St Elizabeth of Hungary prayed when she received news that her young husband (they were married when hardly more than boy and girl) had died while on his way to the Crusade: 'You know, O Lord, that I loved him more than anything in this world, because he loved you and because he was my husband. Since it has pleased You to take him to Yourself, I am perfectly resigned to Your holy will. And if by saying one Our Father I could recall him to life against Your will, I would not say it. Only this I ask: grant unto him eternal rest and to me grace to serve you faithfully until my last breath.' These are two instances of a detachment all the more real because they do not seek anything like that icy lack of feeling that some people have held up as being somehow admirable.

Mention has been made of the name of Guéranger, who did so much to restore the liturgy to its proper place, and to revive a monasticism all but extinct. But we might speak of a writer of a different type, who belonged to a time when the monks were again flourishing. This was Dom Columba Marmion, an Irishman who became abbot of Maredsous, writing and speaking after his admission to religion usually in French. His famous ascetical trilogy,

Christ the Life of the Soul, Christ in His Mysteries, and *Christ the Ideal of the Monk,* have become classics, and one might say classics in all of the many languages into which they have been translated. One is astonished at the easy skill with which he interweaves the Scriptures and the Fathers in his books. Yet actually we should be more astonished had he failed to do this, so permeated was his spiritual life with this rich reading, yet all of it interwoven with a personal and charming talent. It would be hard indeed to find a spiritual writer who is more rewarding, more intimate, more profound, more practical. His books were addressed to his community, yet despite the title of one of his celebrated works, even that need not be reserved solely for monks. Here is a lucid grace that makes even an *O Altitudo* seem almost simple, but never any touch of the feeling that here are *arcana* which all but specialists had better leave alone. Without putting forward any claim that we find in Marmion exclusively Benedictine characteristics – for that is not so – it is at least true that in him we come across a spirituality completely in the Benedictine tradition. Yet it might also be suggested that that very fact gives writing of this sort its universal appeal.

The Benedictine intention is not to pitch the ideal so high as to put it virtually beyond reach. Nor is it to water down the religious concept but merely to affirm that it need not be confined to experts and specialists. To attempt more might result in discouragement, in fact to make extravagant demands could be either hypocritical or ill advised, for human nature is so constituted as to be incapable of being kept perpetually on the summits it may occasionally reach. But to all Christians comes the call, 'My son, give me your heart.' And to all Benedictines,

whether monks or nuns or merely oblates, come the
words with which the Prologue to the Holy Rule opens:
'Hearken, O my son, to the precepts of your master, and
incline the ear of your heart: willingly receive and faithfully fulfil the admonition of your loving father, that you
may return by the labour of obedience to Him from
whom you had departed by the sloth of disobedience.'
The assumption is not that of malice but of negligence: to
a reasonable amount of good will is promised no quick
attainment of dazzling heights, but a steady progress
toward perfection.

Bishop Hedley in his Introduction to Abbot Tosti's
St Benedict says: 'Perhaps the less a monk thinks about
converting the world and the more he thinks about converting himself, the more likely will it be that the world
will be converted.' This is not a disparagement of the
apostolic spirit but is intended merely to indicate that it
operates among Benedictines quietly, naturally, still more
without any fuss or fanfare. The spirit of St Benedict is
one of simplicity and serenity; well might his monks take
as their motto the single word *Pax*. Here rests the blessing
of Benedict.

Brief Bibliography

Benedict, St. *The Holy Rule of Our Most Holy Father Benedict* (8th ed.) Atchison, Kansas. 1935. (See also Delatte, and McCann)

Brémond, Henri. *The Thundering Abbot*. New York, 1930

Butler, Cuthbert, O.S.B. *Benedictine Monachism*. London and New York, 1919

———. *Ways of Christian Life, Old Spirituality for Modern Men*. London and New York, 1933

———. *Western Mysticism*. London, 1922

Cabrol, Fernand, O.S.B. *Saint Benedict* (trans. by C. M. Antony). London, 1934

Chapman, John, O.S.B. *St Benedict and the Sixth Century*. New York and London, 1929

———. *St Benedict*. New York, 1937

Delatte, Paul, O.S.B. *The Rule of St Benedict; a Commentary* (trans. by Justin McCann, O.S.B.). London, 1921

Dirks, Walter. *The Monk and the World* (trans. by Daniel Coogan). New York, 1954

Gasquet, Aiden, O.S.B. (afterward Cardinal). 'A Sketch of Monastic Constitutional History,' Introduction to Vol. I of the Count de Montalembert's *Monks of the West*. New York and London, 1896

———. *The Mission of St Augustine*. London, 1924

———. *Henry VIII and the English Monasteries*, 2 vols. London, 1888–89

———. *Monastic Life in the Middle Ages*. London, 1922

Hannay, James O. *The Spirit and Origin of Christian Monasticism*. London, 1903

Herwegen, Ildephonsus, O.S.B. *St Benedict* (trans. by Peter Nugent, O.S.B.). London, 1924

Knowles, David, O.S.B. *The Benedictines*. New York, 1930

Lindsay, T. F. *Saint Benedict, His Life and Work*. London, 1949

———. *The Holy Rule for Laymen*. London, 1947

Marmion, Columba, O.S.B. *Christ, the Ideal of the Monk* (trans. by a nun of Tyburn Convent). London, 1922

McCann, O.S.B. *Saint Benedict*. New York, 1937

———. *The Rule of St Benedict* (in Latin and English, with notes). London, 1951

Montalembert, Count de. *The Monks of the West*, 5 vols. London, 1896

Morin, *The Ideal of the Monastic Life Found in the Apostolic Age*. Westminster, Maryland, 1950

Newman, John Henry Cardinal. 'The Benedictine Centuries.' London, in *Historical Sketches*, Vol. II. London, 1872

Rios, Romanus, O.S.B. *Benedictines of Today: Studies in Modern Benedictine Sanctity*. Stanbrook Abbey Press, 1946

Rylandt, I., O.S.B. *St Benedict the Man* (trans. by Patrick Shaughnessy, O.S.B.). St Meinrad, Indiana, 1950

Schmitz, Philibert, O.S.B. *Histoire de l'Ordre de Saint-Benoît*, 6 vols. (2nd ed.). Maredsous Abbey, 1948–49

Schuster, Ildephonsus Cardinal, O.S.B. *Saint Benedict and His Times* (trans. by Gregory J. Roettger, O.S.B.). St Louis and London, 1951

Tosti, Luigi, O.S.B. *St Benedict: an Historical Discourse on His Life* (trans. by William Romuald, O.S.B.). London, 1896

Waddell, Helen. *The Desert Fathers*. London, 1936, New York, 1942

Workman, Herbert B. *The Evolution of the Monastic Ideal*. London, 1913

Index